PEOPLES
of
AFRICA

Ethiopia

Gabon

Gambia

Ghana

Guinea

PEOPLES
of
AFRICA

Volume 4
Ethiopia–Guinea

MARSHALL CAVENDISH
NEW YORK • LONDON • TORONTO • SYDNEY

Marshall Cavendish Corporation
99 White Plains Road
Tarrytown, New York 10591-9001

Reference Edition 2003

Consultants:
Bryan Callahan, Department of History, Johns Hopkins University
Kevin Shillington

Pronunciation Consultant: Nancy Gratton

Contributing authors:
  Fiona Macdonald
  Elizabeth Paren
  Kevin Shillington
  Gillian Stacey
  Philip Steele

Discovery Books
  Managing Editor: Paul Humphrey
  Project Editor: Helen Dwyer
  Text Editor: Valerie J. Weber
  Design Concept: Ian Winton
  Designer: Barry Dwyer
  Cartographer: Stefan Chabluk

Marshall Cavendish
  Editorial Director: Paul Bernabeo
  Editor: Marian Armstrong

The publishers would like to thank the following for their permission to reproduce photographs:
  Robert Estall Photo Library (Carol Beckwith/Angela Fisher: 176, 178, 179, 180, 183; David Coulson: 173); Mary Evans Picture Library (174, 216); Werner Forman Archive (172, 207; British Museum, UK: 212 bottom; Dallas Museum of Art, USA: 189; Entwistle Gallery, London, UK: 193); Hutchison Library (Mick Csaky: 213; Sarah Errington: 177; Juliet Highet: 212 top; Sarah Murray: cover; Bernard Régent: 190; Anna Tully: 204; Leslie Woodhead: 185 top); ICCE Photolibrary (Conrad Aveling: 191, 192; Mark Boulton: 199); Panos Pictures (Ian Cartwright: 222; Pietro Cenini: 184, 186; Caroline Penn: 181; Giacomo Pirozzi: 214, 218, 219, 220, 221; Betty Press: 195, 198; Liba Taylor: 194); Still Pictures (Adrian Arbib/Christian Aid: 185 bottom; Julia Baine: 187; Ron Giling: 182, 203, 208; Heine Pedersen: 170; Jorgen Schytte: 200, 206, 209, 210); Topham Picturepoint (217); Tropix Photographic Library (M. & V. Birley: 205, 211; B. McGrath: 197); Redferns Music Picture Library (Graeme Ewens: 223)

(cover) A forklift truck driver loads containers at the port of Abidjan, Ivory Coast.

Editor's note: Many systems of dating have been used by different cultures throughout history. *Peoples of Africa* uses B.C.E. (Before Common Era) and C.E. (Common Era) instead of B.C. (Before Christ) and A.D. (Anno Domini, "In the Year of the Lord") out of respect for the diversity of the world's peoples.

Library of Congress Cataloging-in-Publication Data

Peoples of Africa.
    p. cm.
  Includes bibliographical references and index.
  Contents: v. 1. Algeria–Botswana — v. 2. Burkina-Faso-Comoros — v. 3. Congo, Democratic Republic of–Eritrea — v. 4. Ethiopia–Guinea — v. 5. Guinea-Bissau–Libya — v. 6. Madagascar–Mayotte — v. 7. Morocco–Nigeria — v. 8. Réunion–Somalia — v. 9. South Africa–Tanzania — v. 10. Togo–Zimbabwe — v. 11. Index.
  ISBN 0-7614-7158-8 (set)
    1. Ethnology—Africa—Juvenile literature. 2. Africa—History—Juvenile literature. 3. Africa—Social life and customs—Juvenile literature. I. Marshall Cavendish Corporation.

GN645 .P33 2000
305.8'0096—dc21

                                              99-088550

  ISBN 0-7614-7158-8 (set)
  ISBN 0-7614-7162-6 (vol. 4)

Printed in Hong Kong

06 05 04 03   6 5 4 3 2

Contents

Ethiopia   170–187
   The Empire of Aksum   171
   Religious Conflicts   172
   Emperors Unite Ethiopia   174
   Haile Selassie Dominates   175
   Opposing the Dergue   176
   Peoples, Languages, and Faiths   177
   Improving Education and Health   181
   Drought in a Fertile Land   181
   People of Rural Areas   182
   People of the Cities   184
   Injera, Wat, Berbere, and *Tej*   185
   Athletes and Game Players   186
   Religious Festivals: Timkat and Maskal   187

Gabon   188–193
   Early Settlers   188
   Europeans and Explorers   189
   After Independence   190
   Okoumé, Oil, and Manganese   191
   Living Day to Day   191
   The Gabonese   192

Gambia   194–199
   Elephants and Great Empires   194
   The Coming of the Europeans   196
   Gambia Today   197
   Life of the People   198

Ghana   200–213
   The Ashanti Kingdom   201
   Slave Traders and Gold Seekers   202
   Nkrumah and Independence   203
   Rawlings in Power   204
   The Peoples of Ghana   205
   Families and Clans   205
   Religions and Festivals   207
   Earning a Living   208
   Corn, Millet, Soup, and Sauces   209
   Homes, New and Old   210
   Health and Education   211
   Music and Dance   213

Guinea   214–223
   Guinea's Past   215
   A Move toward Independence   216
   People, Languages, Faiths   218
   Few Hospitals, Few Schools   220
   Everyday Life   220
   Riches from the Earth   222
   Praising Chiefs and Cattle   223

Glossary   224

Further Reading   226

Index   227

ETHIOPIA

ETHIOPIA IS A LANDLOCKED REPUBLIC IN
NORTHEASTERN AFRICA.

*Ethiopia is one of the most mountainous
countries in Africa. It also includes one of the
hottest, driest, and lowest places on
Earth—the desert region of Danakil.*

*The central highlands are known
as the Ethiopian Plateau. Deep
gorges and wide valleys split
the highlands. Here flow
many rivers, large and
small. There are broad-
leaved forests and open
woodland savannas.*

*To the east, the plateau drops
sharply into the Great Rift Valley,
which forms a string of eight rift lakes.
In the lowlands of the east and south there is
grassland and semidesert.*

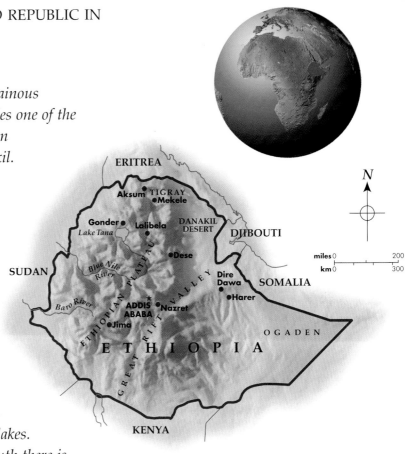

CLIMATE

*The Ethiopian highlands are cooler and wetter
than the lowlands. Night frosts can dust the
mountainous areas, and snow falls on the peaks.
Most rain falls between June and September.*

	Addis Ababa	Harer
Average January temperature:	59°F (15°C)	65°F (18°C)
Average July temperature:	59°F (15°C)	64°F (18°C)
Average annual precipitation:	50 in. (124 cm)	35 in. (90 cm)

*In Ethiopia collecting water is women's work. These women
near Dese (DAE-sae) in the Ethiopian highlands may have to
walk many miles, especially in the years when little rain falls.*

170

The Empire of Aksum

The earliest-known people in Ethiopia (ee-thee-OE-pee-uh) were hunter-gatherers who lived by hunting animals, gathering wild fruits and vegetables, and catching fish in local rivers. Then, probably more than seven thousand years ago, they began farming, learning to grow wild grasses as food crops. Teff, the staple grain of the Ethiopian diet today, was one such wild grass. At about the same time, livestock raising was introduced, probably by peoples who migrated to the region from Asia.

Over a period of about four thousand years, the population of farmers grew in number. They improved their farming methods, settled in small villages and towns, and began trading with people in other towns and regions. Then, in about the sixth century B.C.E., farmers from southwest Arabia (modern Yemen) crossed the Red Sea and set up trading settlements on the coast. They soon intermarried with the local peoples. The Aksum (AHK-soom) Empire emerged from these early developments about two thousand years ago in the northern highlands of Ethiopia.

Today's information about the Aksum Empire comes from both written and archaeological evidence. The empire was first described by the Greeks in the first century C.E. In the third century a Persian writer claimed it was one of the four great kingdoms of the world. For more than five hundred years, it was one of the most important civilizations of its time. Aksum minted its own coins, manufactured glass, copper, and brass goods, and practiced

advanced agriculture, using skillful irrigation techniques.

The Aksumite Empire covered the northern highlands of Ethiopia, controlled the coast of the Red Sea, and, at its height, expanded into part of Arabia. In 350 C.E. it conquered the Meroë Empire in modern-day Sudan (see SUDAN). One of the main reasons why Aksum became so powerful was because it controlled the Red Sea trade routes between India, the Roman Empire,

FACTS AND FIGURES

Official name: *Ityopia*

Status: *Independent state*

Capital: *Addis Ababa*

Major towns: *Dese, Dire Dawa, Gonder, Harer, Jima, Mekele, Nazret*

Area: *471,775 square miles (1,221,897 square kilometers)*

Population: *59,700,000*

Population density: *127 per square mile (49 per square kilometer)*

Peoples: *Main groups are 40 percent Oromo, 40 percent Amhara and Tigre; others include Somali, Gurage, Afar, Sidama, Hareri, Anuak, Nuer*

Official language: *Amharic*

Currency: *Birr*

National days: *Battle of Adwa (March 2); Patriots' Victory Day (May 5); National Day (May 28)*

Country's name: *The country's name probably comes from the Greek word* ethiopic, *meaning "burned faced," and was used to describe the peoples of sub-Saharan Africa.*

Time line:	Hunter-gatherers begin to settle and grow crops	Founding of the Aksum Empire in Ethiopian highlands	Christianity brought by monks from the Roman Empire
	ca. 5000 B.C.E.	ca. 200 C.E.	400s

The Pillars of Aksum

In the northern town of Aksum you can still see the stelae (plural), tall pillars made of solid granite, that adorned the Aksum Empire. The largest stela, which has now fallen, was 108 feet (33 meters) high and weighed approximately 555 tons (500 metric tons). The granite was carried, probably by elephants, from a nearby quarry. Nobody knows how the stelae were lifted into place.

The tallest standing stela is 75 feet (23 meters) high and was probably built in the time of King Ezana in the fourth century C.E. Historians think that stelae were built to show the power of the king; the bigger and more impressive a stela was, the more powerful the king seemed to his people.

The tallest of the still-standing stelae of Aksum. A door and nine windows, believed to symbolize the door and nine chambers in King Ezana's tomb, are carved on it.

and Arabia. Some of the main items it exported were gold, incense, ivory, rhinoceros horn, and obsidian, a black glasslike rock used to make jewelry. Cloth, glass, iron, olive oil, and wine were imported.

The people of Aksum developed a written language called Geez (GIH-ehz), which is still used in the sacred writings of Ethiopian Christianity. Christianity spread widely in the fifth century, when a small group of Christian monks, fleeing persecution in the Roman Empire, arrived in Aksum and began to preach throughout the empire. They built many churches, one of which still remains.

The Aksum Empire began to decline in the seventh century. No one knows exactly why, though different causes have been suggested. The most likely cause was that Muslims from Arabia took control of the Red Sea trade routes.

Religious Conflicts

For many centuries after the decline of Aksum, the Ethiopian highlands were isolated from the outside world. This

Aksum Empire begins to decline	Islam spreads from Red Sea coast	Conflict between Christian Ethiopia and Muslim Adal	Adal conquers large parts of Christian Ethiopia
600s	**1300s**	**1400s**	**1529–1535**

period saw the shaping of the Ethiopian Orthodox Church into a form of Christianity unique to Ethiopia.

From the fourteenth century, Islam spread in the east, moving inland from the Red Sea coast. As more people began to convert to Islam and trade with the Arab world grew, small but powerful Muslim states were established. The most important of these was Adal (uh-DAHL). By the end of the fourteenth century, Adal controlled the main trade routes between the Red Sea coast and the northern plateau of Ethiopia. Ethiopian Christian rulers, who were descended from the Aksum emperors, saw this as a threat to their power—and to their religion—and there were many conflicts between the Christians and Muslims.

Lalibela

Far less famous than the pyramids in Egypt or the city of Petra in Jordan, Lalibela is regarded by many who have visited it as one of the wonders of the world.

In this remote village in the mountains of north-central Ethiopia stand eleven churches hewn from rock. In the thirteenth century the religious King Lalibela hired the best artisans to create beautiful churches in praise of God. The churches were carved from the red mountain rock, and each is unique in the way it is carved and decorated.

The most impressive is probably the Church of Saint George, which is carved in the shape of a cross. Legend tells that Saint George was angry that he was the only saint who did not have a church named after him. King Lalibela promised that the most beautiful of the churches would be his. Locals say that the church still bears the hoofprints of Saint George's horse as he galloped at full speed into the church, either in anger or in joy at the beauty of the building.

The churches of Lalibela are still used regularly for worship. Here, at the beautiful Church of Saint George, Ethiopian Orthodox Christians gather to celebrate the festival of Timkat.

Ethiopians and Portuguese defeat Adal invaders	Ethiopia isolated from rest of world	Modernization and uniting of Ethiopia under Emperors Tewodros and Yohannis IV
1543	**mid-1600s–1850s**	**1855–1889**

During the sixteenth century, a soldier in the Adal army, Ahmad ibn Ibrahim al Ghazi, took control of Adal and the city of Harer in the eastern highlands. He went on to conquer large parts of Christian Ethiopia. About the same time, the first contact was made between Europe and Ethiopia when an expedition from Portugal reached the highlands. The Christian emperor of Ethiopia appealed to the Portuguese for help, and together their forces defeated the Muslims and killed Ahmad. Christian armies gradually took back control of the Ethiopian highlands.

The Portuguese hoped to increase their control over the trade routes to the east, particularly to India. Portuguese Catholic missionaries arrived, but their attempts to persuade Ethiopians to abandon their Orthodox Christianity led to conflict between those who converted to Catholicism and those who stayed true to the Orthodox Church. It created such bitterness that all foreign Roman Catholics were thrown out of Ethiopia in the mid-seventeeth century. For nearly two hundred years, foreigners were no longer welcome in Ethiopia, and the kingdom was once again isolated from the rest of the world.

Emperors Unite Ethiopia

In the middle of the nineteenth century, Ethiopia was not a united country. There was still an emperor, but he had little power over local princes and warlords, who squabbled and fought with one another. The uniting and modernization of Ethiopia began under Emperor Tewodros and was continued by Yohannis IV and Menelik II.

Tewodros fought successfully against other Ethiopian princes, and in 1855 he had himself crowned emperor. He was determined to unite Ethiopia as one country, but his ruthlessness made him unpopular. In 1868, after

A depiction of two men from Emperor Menelik II's guard. These soldiers carried the latest guns plus traditional shields and swords. Their fearsome headgear was made from a lion's mane.

Menelik II rules Ethiopia; establishes the modern borders of Ethiopia	Ethiopians defeat invading Italians at Battle of Adwa	Emperor Haile Selassie rules	Italian conquest of Ethiopia
1889–1913	**1896**	**1930–1974**	**1935–1941**

an argument with British diplomats, Tewodros imprisoned several British people. The British sent thousands of soldiers to rescue the captives. Deserted by his army, Tewodros took his own life.

Yohannis IV also worked to achieve unity by military means, but he was a more diplomatic ruler. He negotiated with Egypt and the European powers to gain recognition of Ethiopian independence.

Menelik II ruled from 1889 to 1913 and finally established the borders of Ethiopia as it exists today, moving the capital to Addis Ababa (AHD-dis AH-bah-bah). This emperor also modernized Ethiopia by introducing electricity, schools and hospitals, telephones and railroads. Menelik's skills as a leader were one of the main reasons why Ethiopia was the only African country to remain free and independent during the European scramble to conquer Africa during the nineteenth and twentieth centuries.

Ethiopian independence was, however, threatened by the Italians. Unlike other more powerful European nations, Italy had no African colonies and hoped to gain a foothold in Africa by colonizing Ethiopia. In 1890 Menelik signed a treaty with the Italians in which he gave them the northern part of Ethiopia, which is now Eritrea (see ERITREA). In return Italy agreed to recognize Ethiopia as an independent kingdom. The Italians had no real intention of sticking to the treaty, and in 1895 they tried to colonize Ethiopia. The result was a disaster for Italy. At the Battle of Adwa in 1896, Menelik's soldiers heavily defeated a well-equipped Italian army.

Haile Selassie Dominates

After Menelik's death his daughter Zauditu became empress. For most of her rule, however, her nephew Ras Tafari was the power behind the throne. After her death in 1930, he became Emperor Haile Selassie.

In 1935 the Italians invaded Ethiopia again. This time they defeated the Ethiopian army and occupied the country. Haile Selassie fled into exile. The Italian occupation was short lived; in 1941 Great Britain (Italy's enemy in World War II) and Haile Selassie, along with Ethiopian patriots from Sudan, defeated the Italians. Ethiopia regained its independence, and Haile Selassie returned to the throne.

As emperor, Haile Selassie was extremely powerful. However, he did very little to develop his country. The peasants lived in great poverty under an ancient feudal system, the power of the rich nobles increased, and little trade or industry was developed. A member of the Amhara people, Selassie also pursued a policy of "Amharisation" of the country, demanding Amhara culture be dominant. The language and culture of other peoples, such as the Oromo and the Tigre, were repressed. This led to resistance in many parts of the country, especially during the 1960s and 1970s. The Eritreans, in particular, fought with great determination to win back their independence, which they had lost in 1962 when Haile Selassie annexed their country (see ERITREA). The aging emperor became increasingly repressive and was eventually overthrown in a military coup in 1974.

Severe droughts and famines	Selassie overthrown; Ethiopia under military rule	Colonel Mengistu Haile Mariam becomes dictator	Rebel forces overthrow Mengistu
1970s–1980s	1974	1977	1991

An Oromo woman sells coffee at market. The Oromo have been excluded from power since the nineteenth century and their culture has been suppressed by Ethiopian governments.

Opposing the Dergue

After the coup, a military committee known as the Dergue took power. The new military rulers wanted to change Ethiopia from a backward, feudal empire to a modern, socialist country. In the beginning the Dergue had popular support, but when they began to force their policies onto the people, opposition grew.

In 1977 a member of the Dergue, Mengistu Haile Mariam, assumed total power. Anyone who opposed him was arrested. Opponents and thousands of ordinary Ethiopians were killed.

In different parts of the country, people organized groups to oppose the government in Addis Ababa. In the northeast the Eritreans and Tigre fought bitterly against Mengistu's army, as did the Somali people in the east. In the mid-1980s the effects of the war and several years of drought caused a terrible famine. Around one million Ethiopians died of starvation.

Several of the rebel groups joined forces to overthrow Mengistu and establish democracy throughout Ethiopia. In 1991 their forces captured Addis Ababa, and Mengistu fled the country.

In 1991 the Eritrean People's Liberation Front entered the Eritrean capital, Asmara (ahz-MAHR-uh), and liberated the country. In 1993 Eritrea became an independent republic (see ERITREA). Recently, however, old border disputes between Ethiopia and Eritrea have flared up, and fighting has once again brought suffering to the people along the border and forced many to flee their villages.

From 1991 onward, Ethiopia moved toward democracy. In 1995 multiparty democratic elections took place, and Ethiopia became a federation of nine regional states. However, Ethiopia still has problems. It remains difficult to balance all the different ethnic groupings, and the economy is fragile. With the exception of Eritrea, which left the federation after a referendum in 1993, Ethiopia has remained united in name, but it is not truly a united country.

Eritrea becomes independent	Multiparty democratic elections won by the Ethiopian People's Revolutionary Democratic Front; federation of nine regional states established	Eritrea and Ethiopia clash over borders
1993	**1995**	**mid-1990s**

Peoples, Languages, and Faiths

Ethiopia is a great mixture of peoples, languages, and cultures. The largest groups are the Amhara (umh-HAH-rah) and Tigre (TEE-grae) of the northern highlands, the Oromo (OE-roe-moe) in central, southern, and eastern Ethiopia, and the Somali (soe-MAH-lee) in the eastern lowlands.

Throughout much of Ethiopia's history, the Amhara have dominated. Almost all Amharic people are Ethiopian Orthodox Christians, and the majority are highland farmers. They speak Amharic, a language that developed from Geez, the ancient language of the Aksum Empire. Probably about 30 percent of the population of Ethiopia speak Amharic as their native tongue.

The power of the Amhara has often caused conflict in Ethiopia. From the time of Menelik until the downfall of the Dergue, the Amhara dominated government and the economy. The culture and languages of other peoples have often been repressed in the name of Ethiopian unity.

The Tigre share many common characteristics

A Tigre man from the Ethiopian Plateau. He wears the traditional highland shemma (SHEH-mah), a robe made from white cotton and worn over the shoulder.

with the Amhara; their language, Tigrinya (tih-GREEN-yah), also developed from Geez. Almost all Tigre are Ethiopian Orthodox Christians, and most are highland farmers. The Tigre are found mostly in the province of Tigray in the northern highlands. Like the Amhara, they have had a strong influence on government and the economy. However, there have also been bitter conflicts with the Amhara.

Since the overthrow of the Dergue, the Tigre have dominated the government of Ethiopia.

The Oromo are the largest group in Ethiopia, estimated to be at least 40 percent of the total population. (There are also a smaller number of Oromo in Kenya.) Their language is called Afan Oromo. Over the last few hundred years, the Oromo have spread throughout southern Ethiopia. Originally nomadic cattle herders, today most are farmers. Small numbers of Oromo still follow their traditional religion, but most are Roman Catholic, Protestant Christian, or Muslim. Many Oromo believe that their regions should form an independent state. Since the time of Menelik II, the Ethiopian government, perhaps fearing their growing numbers, has done all it can to suppress the Oromo way of life.

A nomadic Afar girl, with beaded jewelry and braided hair, from the Danakil Desert. Her filed teeth are considered a sign of beauty among the Afar people.

The Somali live mainly in Somalia, but there are many also living in the Ogaden (oe-GAH-den) region of Ethiopia, a region claimed by Somalia. They speak a language related to that of the Oromo, and many also speak Arabic. Many Somali are nomadic cattle and camel herders, while others are settled farmers. Most Somali are Muslim. It is difficult to estimate their numbers today since many are refugees who have fled from Somalia.

Other peoples include the Afar of the Danakil (DA-nuh-kil) Desert, the Sidama (sih-DAH-mah) in the highlands, the Gurage (goo-RAHJ) in central Ethiopia, the Hareri (huh-RAE-ree) in the east, and the Anuak and Nuer in the southwest and west. There are also refugees from Somalia

and Sudan. In addition, during the worst years of famine and fighting in the 1980s, as many as 1.5 million Ethiopians fled to Somalia and Sudan.

More than eighty languages are spoken in Ethiopia. English is the first foreign language taught in secondary schools, and it is also spoken in business and in colleges and universities.

Most Ethiopians follow either Ethiopian Orthodox Christianity or Islam. Statistics vary and are often unreliable, but each of these two faiths is probably followed by about 40 percent of the population. The rest of the population are Protestant or Roman Catholic Christians, or followers of traditional religions.

Most Orthodox Christians are found in the highlands. Their church is unique. It developed in near isolation from the outside world for a thousand years, and the teachings and practices have changed

The Ethiopian Calendar

Tourist brochures welcome visitors to "Ethiopia—land of thirteen months of sunshine." This is because the Ethiopian calendar is divided into thirteen months. It is a solar calendar, started by Roman Emperor Julius Caesar two thousand years ago. Each year has twelve equal months of thirty days and a thirteenth month of five days. The thirteenth month is six days long every leap year.

The Ethiopian calendar runs seven years behind the Western, or Gregorian, calendar. The first month of the year is Meskerem in September, with New Year's Day being celebrated on September 11th. Thus, September 11, 2000, in the West was New Year's Day 1993 in Ethiopia.

The Ark of the Covenant

According to the Old Testament of both Christians and Jews, the Ark of the Covenant was a sacred chest that contained the tablets of the Ten Commandments, the laws God gave Moses. The Ark was seen as a symbol of God's presence among his chosen people, and it was believed to be so holy and powerful that to merely touch it was punishable by death. The Old Testament tells how it was carried by the Israelites during their wanderings in the wilderness and then placed in the Great Temple built by King Solomon. The Babylonians burned the temple in 587 B.C.E., and the Ark disappeared, never to be seen again.

Ethiopian Orthodox Christians believe that the Ark was taken to Ethiopia during the time of the Aksum Empire and is now kept in a church in the modern town of Aksum. The Ark is locked away and hidden from human sight. The only person alive who is said to have seen the Ark is the official guardian of the church.

The presence of the Ark in Aksum may only be legend, but Ethiopian Christians believe it is there. For them it is the most powerful symbol of God on Earth.

regular days of fasting. Orthodox Christians recognize both the Jewish Sabbath on Saturday and the Christian Sabbath on Sunday.

Every Orthodox church has an inner chamber for relics or holy objects. Only the priest may enter the chamber. The holiest object is the *tabot* (TAH-boe), a replica of the Ark of the Covenant. The tabot is taken from the church only on important religious days. Hidden from

Young deacons of the Orthodox Church celebrating Genna (Ethiopian Christmas). They wear filigree crowns and embroidered capes. One carries a finely carved gold cross.

little, even at the beginning of the twenty-first century. The basic teachings are clearly Christian, but the rituals retain many ancient Jewish influences that have been lost to other branches of Christianity. For example, infant boys are circumcised only a few days after birth, and there are

A heavily veiled Muslim woman, one of the nomadic lowland Rashaida (ruh-SHAE-dah) people, on her wedding day. Her long wedding veil is made of silver and gold.

traditional religion, the supreme god is called Waka and he is represented by spirits on Earth. These spirits can be contacted through a ritual priest, who may be possessed by them.

view by a cloth, it is carried on the head of a priest in a procession.

Muslims are found throughout Ethiopia, but most are concentrated in the east and southeast. The strictest followers of the faith usually live in the larger towns. In rural areas and among nomadic peoples, such as the Afar, the religion is not always strictly followed.

Believers in traditional religions are scattered through parts of the south and southwest. Although they have different practices, almost all believe in one supreme god. This god is distant from the everyday life of ordinary people and is usually addressed through spirits. Among those Oromo who continue to follow their

The Falasha

Falasha *(fuh-LAH-shuh) is the Amharic word for "stranger," and it is used to describe a group of Ethiopian Jews who believe they are descended from the son of King Solomon and the Queen of Sheba. The Falasha probably entered the Ethiopian highlands as traders around the beginning of the first millennium* C.E. *They call themselves* Beta Israel *(BAE-tah IHZ-rah-ehl), meaning "House of Israel," and they follow all the religious practices of the Jewish faith. In their synagogues they read the Old Testament of the Bible in Geez.*

The Falasha played an important part in the early history of Ethiopia, but they have suffered greatly during the twentieth century. Until the 1980s there were probably about thirty thousand Falasha living in isolated villages north of Lake Tana (TAH-nah). During the 1970s and 1980s they suffered famines and became caught up in the civil war. Many fled to Sudan. Almost all the Falasha were airlifted to Israel in three rescue operations from 1984 to 1991. The operations were organized by the Israeli government, which recognized their right to Israeli citizenship. Today there are hardly any Falasha left in Ethiopia, just a few small isolated communities in remote mountain areas.

Improving Education and Health

The literacy rate in Ethiopia is low; only about one-third of the population can read and write. Children in large cities are much more likely to have the opportunity to attend school than those in rural areas. In recent years there have been major campaigns to expand education, especially for children of elementary-school age. In most elementary and secondary schools, children are taught in their local language.

Life expectancy in Ethiopia averages forty-one years. Many people live in isolated areas where few modern health facilities are available. Villagers often rely on traditional healers and herbal medicine. Most Ethiopian women undergo the practice of female genital cutting (see SOMALIA). In recent years the government has tried hard to improve community health, including training health workers

A health worker talks to villagers in the Gonder (GAWN-duhr) region. There are few proper health facilities in rural areas, so health education is especially important.

and birth attendants, but, as Ethiopia remains a very poor country, problems with funding health services continue.

Drought in a Fertile Land

A large number of Ethiopians live by farming. The most widely grown crop is teff, a grain used to make *injera*, the staple food in the Ethiopian diet. Coffee, another widely grown crop, is believed to have originated in Ethiopia. It is the country's main export crop today. Ethiopians also raise large numbers of livestock, including cattle, sheep, and goats.

The processing of raw agricultural products is one of the few industries in Ethiopia. Gold and iron are mined but only in small quantities. Salt is also mined. It is hoped that electricity may be produced in the future, using geothermal and hydroelectric power from the springs and lakes of the southern Great Rift Valley.

In the 1980s Ethiopia made the world's headlines when one million people died in a terrible famine. Drought caused a crop

181

failure, and the war in the country prevented people from buying and selling food. Many people were forced to leave their land and become refugees. They suffered terrible hunger, malnutrition, and sickness. They only survived through the distribution of food donated by other countries.

The television scenes of starving children led many people in prosperous countries in Europe and North America to think of Ethiopia only as a land of famine. However, much of the farmland in the highlands is extremely fertile. When there is enough rain, the harvests can be very good. In 1997, for example, Ethiopia had a food surplus in many farming areas and exported corn to Kenya.

People of Rural Areas

Nearly 90 percent of all Ethiopians live in rural areas. The extended family (closely related people of several generations) and the clan (all people who share a common ancestor) are at the heart of everyday life. For people whose lives are often hard and uncertain, family, clan, and religion provide a sense of belonging and security.

The geography of Ethiopia means that most people live fairly isolated lives. They may travel to nearby villages or towns, but they rarely come into contact with outsiders. Therefore, highland peoples

A farmer using the age-old method of plowing with a simple wooden plow and oxen. Few farmers in Ethiopia have enough land or money to afford a tractor.

182

know little of the way of life of lowland peoples.

Until the 1970s, an ancient form of land ownership prevented most Ethiopians from owning their own land. Under this feudal system, almost all land belonged to nobles or landlords, and the peasant farmers rented what little land they could afford. They had to pay taxes and provide labor to the nobles and to the church.

During the time of the Dergue, the government took control of the land. The peasant farmer still had no rights. Many were forced to leave their villages and settle in unfamiliar areas, far from their family homes. Today the situation is changing, but slowly. The government still controls the land but allows families the right to hand down land they farm to their children.

In highland villages families live in *tukuls* (TOO-kuhls), houses made of stone with thatched roofs, and daily life revolves around farming. They use simple plows to farm the land and grow grains such as teff. Life in the villages often involves going to the local markets and attending church.

In the highlands both men and women wear the traditional *shemma*, a length of white cotton cloth. For women it is worn as a dress, often with a gauzelike white fabric wrapped around it. On special occasions women wear dresses with highly embroidered borders. For men the shemma is worn like a robe draped over the shoulders.

In the southwestern lowlands, near the Sudan border, live the Anuak and the Nuer. The Anuak (AHN-oo-ahk) are tall, lean, and very dark skinned. They live in large villages near rivers such as the Baro (BAHR-oe). They build houses of thatch, with plaster floors made of mud and cow manure. They live by fishing in the rivers and farming. Rivers play a central part in their lives. They provide drinking water

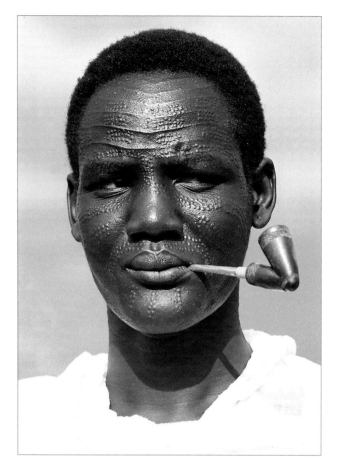

A man from the seminomadic Nuer people. His face is decorated with distinctive Nuer scars, the result of many deliberate small cuts in the skin.

and water for bathing and washing clothes. Most local travel is done on the rivers in dugout canoes.

The Nuer (NOO-uhr) are shorter but also very dark skinned. They are cattle keepers who live a seminomadic life. They make temporary settlements and move on with their cattle when more grazing is needed (see SUDAN).

The Afar (uh-FAHR), nomadic herders of the Danakil Desert, have always known how to survive in one of the most hostile places on earth (see DJIBOUTI). Their homes are tents. Camels provide transportation, and their herds of cattle, goats, and sheep provide meat and milk. Today many Afar are leaving the desert to live in cities, such as Addis Ababa and Djibouti, where almost 80 percent are unemployed.

People of the Cities

The towns and cities of Ethiopia can show contrasting lifestyles. For example, the city of Harer (HAHR-uhr) in the east is hundreds of years old, while the capital city, Addis Ababa, is quite modern.

The walled city of Harer is the spiritual heart of Ethiopia's Muslim community and is regarded as the fourth holiest Islamic city in the world. It has nearly one hundred mosques, a huge number for such a small area. Many of these are private and used just for family worship.

The Hareri (huh-RAE-ree) people have their own language, customs, and way of dressing. Traditionally, Hareri women wear bright velvet pants and cover their heads with fine veils. The name *Hareri* means "people of the city," but there are also Hareri who live in the countryside around the city and who farm small plots of land.

Within the walls of the old city lies a maze of cobbled streets with flat-roofed stone-and-plaster houses. Most of these houses consist of an open room on the ground floor with a raised, carpeted area, where people socialize and guests are entertained. The walls are decorated with brightly colored baskets and pots. Large stone steps serve as chairs, tables, and beds.

Trade is an important part of life in Harer. There are separate markets for Muslims and Christians. This results partly from a time when only Muslims lived in Harer and partly because the different faiths have different ways of preparing their food.

Addis Ababa, established as Ethiopia's capital by Emperor Menelik II about one hundred years ago, is very different from Harer. The population of Addis Ababa is estimated to be about 1.5 million people. The inhabitants are a great mixture of people who have moved there from villages throughout Ethiopia. Amharic, Oromo, and Gurage people are in the majority.

Addis Ababa is a city of contrasts; stylish modern buildings stand near

One of the markets in Harer. In the background are the typical flat-roofed stone-and-plaster houses and the minaret of one of the city's many mosques.

Children playing soccer in Addis Ababa. The backdrop of high-rise buildings, street lighting, and wide roads shows the modern, international face of the capital.

unplanned squatter settlements. The Organization of African Unity and the United Nations Economic Commission for Africa both have their headquarters here, resulting in a large international community. Over fifty thousand people from other countries in Africa and different parts of the world live here.

Most of the local people live in poor housing and have no running water or electricity. Approximately 30 percent are unemployed, and many beggars work the streets. Nevertheless, there are more school and health facilities here than elsewhere in Ethiopia.

Addis Merkato, the main market in Addis Ababa, is the trading heart of the city and covers an area of several square miles. Coffee has its own market within the Merkato; 150 varieties of coffee bean are offered here.

A woman makes injera for the family meal. The dough, made from teff, is first fermented for up to three days. This gives injera its characteristic sour taste and rubbery texture.

Injera, Wat, Berbere, **and** *Tej*

At the heart of Ethiopian food is *injera* (ihn-JEH-rah), a flat sourdough pancake made from teff. Injera is usually served with a vegetable or meat stew called *wat* (WAHT). Ethiopians like their stews hot and spicy and use a special blend of spices known as *berbere* (beh-BEH-reh). This may include up

185

People eat with their right hand, tearing off pieces of injera and using it to scoop up pieces of meat or sauce. Guests are offered the tastiest pieces of meat.

With an Ethiopian meal, people often drink a local beer or *tej* (TEHJ), a kind of wine made from honey. Coffee is also widely drank.

A wall painting from a fifteenth-century church near Lake Tana. Murals showing religious images and scenes of medieval Ethiopian life cover the church walls.

to fifteen different spices, but the main spice is almost always hot chili pepper.

Vegetarian stews are normally eaten on fasting days in the Christian Orthodox Church. These may include beans, peas, lentils, or vegetables such as spinach and red onions.

The main meat is beef, eaten cooked, dried, or raw. In the highlands, people also consume mutton (the flesh of a mature sheep) and in the lowlands goat or camel meat is eaten.

Before a traditional Ethiopian meal, a jug of water and soap is brought in for people to wash their hands. Everyone eats together from one large circular plate.

Athletes and Game Players

Ethiopia is famous for its long-distance runners. A frequent record breaker, Haile Gebre Selassie is regarded by many as the greatest long-distance runner of all time. He won a gold medal in the 10,000-meter race at the 1996 Atlanta Olympics. Fatuma Roba also won a gold medal in the 1996 Olympic marathon and in 1997 was the first African woman to win the Boston Marathon. Soccer, horseracing, and wrestling are also popular sports.

In rural areas, people play a board game called *gabata* (gah-BAH-tah) in which pebbles are dropped in holes.

Chat

A popular pastime throughout Ethiopia is chewing chat *(SHAT). Chat is a green, bitter-tasting leaf that has the effect of a mild stimulant. It is chewed, often for hours on end, in the company of friends. Chewing chat is seen as a great social activity. Chat is especially popular among Muslims who are forbidden to drink alcohol.*

Religious Festivals: Timkat and Maskal

Festivals are an important feature of Ethiopian life, especially religious festivals in the Ethiopian Orthodox Church. The most important of these is Timkat, the Feast of Epiphany, which takes place on January 19. The feast celebrates the baptism of Jesus by John the Baptist. Everyone wears their best clothes. The priests are dressed in their ceremonial clothes, made of velvet or satin and embroidered with bright sequins. Beer and tej are brewed, special food is cooked, and children are given gifts. There are colorful processions, feasting, singing, and dancing.

On the eve of Timkat, the priests bring the tabots from their churches, which are carried in procession to the nearest river. People camp out while the priests pray through the night. As dawn breaks, priests sprinkle water on the faithful, recalling the baptism of Jesus. Some followers jump fully clothed into the river to show the strength of their faith.

Another important festival is Maskal, the Finding of the True Cross, which takes place on September 27. This celebrates what Ethiopians believe to be the discovery of the cross on which Jesus was crucified. On the evening before the festival, yellow daisies are tied at the top of tree branches. These branches are then burned to recall the legend of Empress Helena, who, it is said, found the True Cross. She burned incense and prayed to God to show her the Holy Sepulchre, the tomb where Jesus was buried. When she dug at the place where the smoke from the incense drifted, she found three crosses. One was believed to be the True Cross.

Orthodox Christians gather to celebrate the Timkat festival in Gonder. Priests move in procession through the heart of the crowd. The umbrellas provide shade from the midday sun.

GABON

G ABON LIES ON THE EQUATOR, in western central Africa. It is bordered in
the west by the Atlantic Ocean.

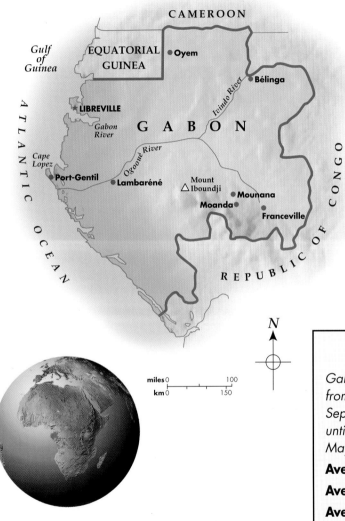

*Lagoons and estuaries indent Gabon's
coastline. The chief waterway is the
Ogooué River, which crosses
wetlands to reach the Atlantic
Ocean south of Port-Gentil. The
capital, Libreville, is located on a
great inlet known as the Gabon
River. Nearly three-quarters of
the country is covered in lush
equatorial forest. There are small
pockets of grassland, the largest in
the far east. Most of the interior is
plateau country, rising to 5,167 feet
(1,575 meters) at Mount Iboundji.*

CLIMATE

*Gabon is hot and humid. A dry season extends
from May to September, a rainy season from
September until December, a second dry season
until mid-February, and then heavy rains fall until
May.*

Average January temperature: *80°F (27°C)*

Average July temperature: *75°F (24°C)*

Average annual precipitation: *99 in. (251 cm)*

Early Settlers

Settlement in Gabon (gah-BOEN) goes back
many thousands of years. Tools and
pottery dating back to the Late Stone Age
have been found. The aboriginal peoples of
the region were of small stature. A few
thousand of their descendants, the Baka
(BAH-kah) people, still live in the forests
around the Ivindo River in the northeast
(see CAMEROON and CONGO, REPUBLIC OF).

The early history of Gabon is marked by
shifting populations. Bantu-speaking
peoples first migrated into the region
probably around 500 B.C.E., and by about
100 C.E. they had begun making and using
iron. By the 1400s the Loango Kingdom of
the Vili people extended into southern
Gabon (see CONGO, REPUBLIC OF). This
became part of the great medieval empire

of Kongo, with its power base far to the south in Angola (see ANGOLA and CONGO, DEMOCRATIC REPUBLIC OF). By the 1500s the Myene (mee-AE-nae) peoples were established along the northern coast, the Orungu (oe-ROON-goo) around Cape Lopez, and the Mpongwe (uhm-PAWN-gwae) on the Gabon River. No large empires could develop in the dense rain forests. The 1600s and 1700s saw further Bantu immigration as Fang (FAHN-jee) people entered Gabon from the north.

FACTS AND FIGURES

Official name: *République Gabonaise*

Status: *Independent state*

Capital: *Libreville*

Major towns: *Port-Gentil, Franceville*

Area: *102,317 square miles (265,001 square kilometers)*

Population: *1,200,000*

Population density: *12 per square mile (5 per square kilometer)*

Peoples: *36 percent Fang; 25 percent Mbede (including Mbete, Teke); 22 percent Eshira; 17 percent other*

Official language: *French*

Currency: *CFA franc*

National day: *Independence Day (August 17)*

Country's name: *The word Gabon comes from the Portuguese* gabão, *meaning "hooded cloak," the shape of the coastline around the Gabon River, according to early explorers.*

A Deadly Dance

The Bantu peoples were masters of ironworking. The traditional weapons of the Fang and the Kota (KOE-tah) peoples were deadly but beautifully crafted. Curved, sicklelike knives were made for throwing. They had finely edged iron blades about 12 inches (30 centimeters) long. Knives were used in warfare as well as in risky ritual dances, where the dancers had to leap over the moving blades.

Europeans and Explorers

As early as 1472, the Portuguese had sailed into the mouth of the Gabon River, and soon Europeans were trading in ivory and slaves along the coast. Local peoples sent prisoners of war and criminals into slavery and capitalized on this cruel trade, which broke up families, removed those people able to work, and thus destroyed whole communities.

During the 1800s the British were increasing their commercial strength around the Gulf of Guinea (GIH-nee). Their rivals,

Time line:	Forest peoples inhabit the region	Bantu-speakers spread farming settlements throughout the region	European trade in slaves and ivory begins	Fang people move in from north	Freed slaves found Libreville
	ca. 1000 B.C.E.	ca. 500 B.C.E.–100 C.E.	1500s C.E.	1600–1700s	1849

the French, wanted a share of trade, and between 1838 and 1842 they signed treaties with Mpongwe kings to gain territory around the Gabon River. Around the same time, Christian missionaries arrived, and the slave trade was brought to an end. Freed slaves founded the city of Libreville (LEE-bruh-vil) in 1849. In 1880 the town of Franceville was established in the far southeast, and in 1889 Gabon was united with the French colony of Mid-Congo (today's Republic of Congo).

Women supporting the Parti Démocratique Gabonais during the 1990 elections wear dresses decorated with pictures of Omar Bongo, Gabon's long-standing president.

In 1910 the French united their colonies in the region to form French Equatorial Africa. Private franchises were issued to companies, which began to exploit the great forests for their timber. They exploited the people, too, with forced labor that was little better than slavery. Whole communities were forced to move into forest areas to collect rubber and other forest products. Many died of malnutrition and disease.

After Independence

During the 1940s and 1950s, the people of Gabon formed political parties and in 1960 achieved independence from France. The first president was Léon M'ba. His party, the Bloc Démocratique Gabonais (BDG), formed a coalition with the opposition, Union Démocratique et Sociale Gabonaise (UDSG). However, the UDSG leader, Jean-Hilaire Abaume, staged a coup in 1964. French troops were sent in to restore M'ba to power.

M'ba died three years later, and the pro-French Albert-Bernard (later Omar) Bongo became president. In 1968 Gabon became a one-party state ruled by Bongo's Parti Démocratique Gabonais (PDG). Bongo wasted vast sums of foreign aid. Among other extravagances, he built a presidential palace at the cost of $120 million.

Opposition against Bongo grew during the 1980s. In 1990 multiparty elections were held, which the PDG won, but the elections were widely believed to have been rigged. Widespread riots and protests raged. Unrest continued after the 1993 election. In 1994, Bongo allowed opposition politicians to join the government. In 1996 the PDG was reelected.

Gabon joined with Mid-Congo	Gabon becomes part of French Equatorial Africa	Independence from France	One-party state	Multiparty elections; riots and protests	Bongo and Parti Démocratique Gabonais reelected
1889	1910	1960	1968–1990	1990	1996

Okoumé, Oil, and Manganese

Although Gabon has economic problems, it is rich in resources. Its rain forests produce Gabon mahogany (*okoumé*), walnut, ebony, and many other species known by African names. Softwoods are exported for use in manufacturing plywood, and hardwoods are sold for furniture making.

Oil is the country's chief export. The Rabi-Kounga oil field has been fully functional since 1990. Large numbers of workers from other African countries come to Gabon to seek work in the oil industry, but most of the oil wealth goes to the favored city dwellers of Libreville and Port-Gentil (pawr-zhan-TEE). Uranium is mined around Moanda (MWAHN-dah), and manganese reserves in the Mounana region are some of the largest in the world. Huge reserves of iron ore wait to be tapped around Bélinga. Three-quarters of the country's energy needs are met by hydroelectric projects. Industry is largely foreign owned.

During the 1980s the Trans-Gabon railroad, which runs from the coast near Libreville to Franceville, was opened, exposing the rain forests to further logging. Torrential seasonal rains hinder travel by road, and people paddle along the rivers in dugout canoes called pirogues.

Sixty-four percent of the Gabonese labor force work on the land, but Gabon has so much dense rain forest that little land is left for agriculture. Sugarcane forms the chief cash crop. Families grow cassava (a starchy root), corn, bananas, and yams.

Living Day to Day

Gabonese food is typical of the region. It consists largely of a stiff porridge called *fufu* (FOO-foo), which is made of cornmeal or cassava and served with a vegetable or meat sauce. People still hunt large animals such as monkeys, antelopes, and crocodiles in the forests. Along the coast and rivers, fishing also provides food.

In many parts of the country, people live in houses made from traditional materials; wall posts are covered in dried mud, roofs are thatched, and reed matting serves as doors and shutters. However, concrete and sheet metal are increasingly used for building materials.

Libreville is a modern city with high-rise office buildings and hotels and wide, traffic-filled avenues. It is home to many wealthy expatriate Europeans. Libreville is

A guenon monkey falls victim to a hunter. Monkeys have always been hunted in western and central Africa, but recently the survival of several species has been threatened.

191

A hot Sunday afternoon in Libreville means escape to the seaside. Gabonese go to the capital's beaches to stroll, meet friends, or swim in the Atlantic Ocean.

an expensive city to live in. It is an attraction to many young people from the countryside, and it has had a university since the 1970s.

The education system has improved greatly since independence; ten years of education are compulsory. Sixty percent of Gabonese can read and write. About one-third can speak French. Of the many Bantu languages, Fang is the most widespread.

The Kola Nut

The kola is a dark brown nut about the size of a chestnut. It comes from two species of evergreen tree native to tropical Africa. Kola nuts are collected and dried. They contain caffeine (the active ingredient of coffee), and despite their bitter taste, they are chewed as a stimulant. In Gabon and throughout most of western Africa, the gift of a kola nut is seen as a token of friendship or hospitality.

Gabon's health system has been well funded by the government in recent years, but it has to grapple with AIDS, leprosy, malaria, cholera, and yellow fever. Life expectancy is fifty-four for men and fifty-seven for women.

The Gabonese

Almost all Gabonese are Bantu-speaking people. There are about forty distinct, small, ethnic groups. The Myene peoples, who includes the Mpongwe and Orungu, live along the northern coasts. The Myene gained power and influence from occupying the lands around the Gabon River. These lands became a center of trade and, later, a center for the colonial administration. The most numerous ethnic group is that of the Fang, which accounts for more than one-third of the population. Fang also live across the border in Cameroon and Equatorial Guinea,

Let's Talk Fang

mbole (uhm-BOE-leh)	*good day*
wa ne mvé? (wah-nehm-VEH)	*you are well?* *(how are you?)*
mé ne mvé (meh-nehm-VEH)	*I'm well*
abora (AH-boe-rah)	*thanks*
mé ka (MAE-kah)	*good-bye*

numbering over three million in all (see CAMEROON and EQUATORIAL GUINEA). The Gabonese Fang mostly live north of the Ogooué (oe-goe-WAE) River.

South of the Ogooué are the Eshira (eh-SHEE-rah), Panu (PAH-noo), Nzebi (ehn-ZAE-bee), and Mbete (uhm-BAE-tee). The Benge (BEHN-gae) and Seke (SAE-kae) live in the far northwest of Gabon, the Kota and Teke (TAE-kae) in the east (see CONGO, REPUBLIC OF). President Omar Bongo belongs to the Teke and has succeeded in gaining support from other ethnic groups in order to exclude the largest single group, the Fang, from power.

Most of these Bantu peoples share similar traditions and customs. Families were often grouped together in clans; all members of a clan could claim descent from the same male ancestor. Rituals honoring ancestors were important, and wooden statues or chests called reliquaries contained the skulls or bones of important ancestors. Fang reliquaries were carved in wood, while the Kota used copper or brass.

Many of the peoples of Gabon used masks in rituals or while making music with drums and xylophones. Fang masks were often black and white, while the Mpongwe wore white masks to communicate with their ancestors; symbolically white was the color of death.

For many peoples of the region, life began to change rapidly during the twentieth century as they gave up farming or hunting for industrial or plantation work or moved to the cities. Wood carving no longer forms a part of everyday life.

However, religious traditions do survive. While the majority of people are Christian, following Roman Catholic or Protestant teachings, many still follow African religions. Many Fang and related peoples believe in the power of spirits, often those of ancestors or those who can be reached through the spirits of ancestors.

Communication with spirits is aided by the use of a powerful hallucinogenic drug called *iboga* (ee-BOE-gah), which is made from the root of a shrub. The people believe that these spiritual powers can be used by witches to cause evil or to harm individuals. Healers try to counter this evil and search out the witches. Each cult centers around a shrine, where people go to be cleansed of evil spirits.

A hundred years ago many beautifully carved heads called bieri *(bee-YEHR-ee) were attached to bark reliquaries as guardians of the bones. People honored their ancestors by making offerings.*

193

GAMBIA

GAMBIA IS THE SMALLEST INDEPENDENT STATE IN MAINLAND AFRICA. It lies on Africa's west coast and, except for its western border on the Atlantic Ocean, is completely surrounded by Senegal.

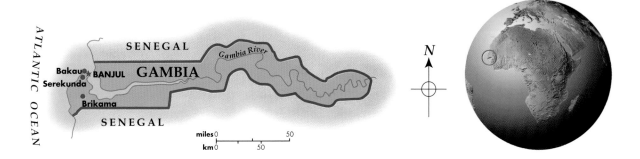

The country forms a narrow strip, 15 to 30 miles (24 to 48 kilometers) wide and 200 miles (320 kilometers) long, which runs along either side of the Gambia River. Most of the land is floodplain. Mangrove swamps grow on the lower reaches of the river. Savanna vegetation can be found on the few low hills.

Most people in Gambia are Muslim, and a mosque stands in every village. Sometimes it may be as richly decorated as this one.

CLIMATE

The country has a subtropical climate. The dry, cooler season runs from November to May. The dry harmattan wind from the Sahara often blows in January and February, bringing a thick red dust. During the wet season, which lasts from June to October, humidity is high and the temperature can reach 90°F (32°C). The rainfall usually takes the form of torrential downpours with high winds.

Average January temperature: *72°F (22°C)*

Average July temperature: *84°F (29°C)*

Average annual precipitation: *51 in. (130 cm)*

Elephants and Great Empires

The first written references to the Gambia (GAM-bee-uh) region were in the works of Hanno, a traveler from northern Africa. Around 500 B.C.E. he told stories of his encounters with elephants and hippos along the Gambia River. Herodotus, a Greek historian writing in 445 B.C.E., remarked how the people of the area made wine from the sap of palm trees.

When looking at the early history of the region, it is easier to think of Gambia and Senegal together as Senegambia (seh-ni-GAM-bee-uh). For many centuries this area was affected by the rise and fall of empires that were based farther east. From about the 400s to the 1200s C.E., Senegambia was part of the empire of Ghana. The principal people of Ghana were the Soninke (soe-NIHN-keh). Some migrated westward and today can be found in Gambia, where they are called the Serahuli (seh-rah-HOO-lee). During the 1200s the Mali Empire dominated western Africa. The leaders of this empire were the Malinke (muh-LIHN-kee). They, like the Soninke, were part of

FACTS AND FIGURES

Official name: *Republic of The Gambia*

Status: *Independent state*

Capital: *Banjul*

Other towns: *Bakau, Brikama, Serekunda*

Area: *4,003 square miles (10,368 square kilometers)*

Population: *1,300,000*

Population density: *325 per square mile (125 per square kilometer)*

Peoples: *40 percent Malinke (or Mandinka); 20 percent Fulani; 14 percent Wolof; 10 percent Jola; 9 percent Serahuli; also Serer and Aku*

Official language: *English*

Currency: *Dalasi*

National day: *Independence Day (February 18)*

Country's name: *Gambia possibly comes from* cambio, *which is Spanish for "exchange," reflecting its historical importance as a trading center.*

the larger Mandingo ethnic group. Some Malinke traders began moving into Senegambia in the 1200s.

Already in Senegambia at that time were the Wolof (WOE-lawf) and the Serer (seh-REHR) peoples, living in agricultural communities along the northern bank of the Gambia River. From the 1000s onward there were also groups of Fulani (foo-LAH-

This woman belongs to the Fulani ethnic group. In Gambia many Fulani have given up their nomadic way of life to become settled farmers or workers in the towns.

Time line:	Empire of Ghana flourishes	Mali Empire dominates the region	First Europeans arrive	Treaty of Versailles recognizes Gambia River as British
	ca. 400s–1200s C.E.	ca. 1200s–1400s	1465	1783

nee). Some Fulani groups may have come into the area from the land that is now Guinea to the south. Others originated in Senegal to the north. They were nomads, traveling from pasture to pasture with their cattle. Groups of Fulani people also migrated right across the savanna regions of western Africa.

The Coming of the Europeans

Europeans began showing interest in western Africa in the 1300s, hearing stories of fabulously rich kingdoms. The first European travelers to visit Gambia were the Portuguese in 1465. They traveled up both the Senegal and Gambia Rivers, trading in slaves and gold. Chiefs in the interior, who for a long time had made slaves of their defeated enemies, began trading these slaves to the Portuguese in exchange for imported goods, including guns and horses.

The Portuguese introduced the idea of sending slaves to work in the plantations of the Americas, and the first slave ship traveled from western Africa in 1510.

The Portuguese were soon followed by the English, the Dutch, and the French, all anxious to profit from the western African slave trade. They competed with each other, capturing each other's trading posts. The Treaty of Versailles in 1783 recognized the Gambia River as British territory.

In 1807 Britain abolished the slave trade, and British ships began patrolling the western African coast to stop other countries that still continued the hateful commerce. They needed a naval base for

this work, and in 1816 they took control of Bathurst, now Banjul (BAHN-jool), for this purpose. This was also where they resettled the freed slaves, the people who became known as the Aku (AH-koo).

By 1880 the French had imposed control over Senegal, and Gambia was thus surrounded by French territory. In 1889 the British and French recognized the borders of Gambia, and in 1894 the British declared the territory their protectorate.

While British colonial rule had some impact on Bathurst and the area around it, the chiefs remained in charge in the interior. After World War II (1939–1945), the British brought in experts to increase production of peanuts, the main cash crop of the colony, and built schools and medical facilities. In 1948 citizens in the capital were allowed to vote, but it was 1961 before the people of the interior could do so. In the elections of that year, the People's Progressive Party (PPP), supported mainly by the Malinke people in the interior, won the most seats. Gambia was the last British west African colony to gain independence. This was achieved in 1965 under the leadership of Dawda Jawara of the PPP.

In 1982 cooperation with Senegal was formalized in a confederation between the two countries, but this ended in 1989. In 1994 the military, led by Colonel Yahya Jammeh, seized power. The Alliance for Reorientation and Construction, the name given to the military government, was elected in 1997 under a new constitution, with Jammeh as its leader and president of the country.

British establish naval base at Bathurst	British declare a protectorate over Gambia	Gambia becomes independent	Confederation with Senegal	Military takeover	Yahya Jammeh elected president
1816	1894	1965	1982–1989	1994	1997

Gambia Today

The largest ethnic group in Gambia is the Malinke (sometimes called the Mandinka). Most are farmers who live in the interior and speak their own language. They also live in Senegal (see SENEGAL). The Serahuli, who speak a related language, live along the reaches of the upper river, near the border. Some are farmers and some are traders. The Serer also live along the riverbanks as farmers in small scattered communities and across the border in Senegal (see SENEGAL).

Many Wolof are farmers too, living along the riverbanks in compact villages. In Banjul live Wolof traders. Their language is commonly used by all those engaged in commerce. In neighboring Senegal, more than one-third of the people are Wolof. In the past the Wolof belonged to one of ten castes, or classes. The most important people were the aristocracy; below them were the warriors, then members of craft guilds, peasants, and servants; at the bottom of the social scale came the slaves. Proposed marriages between members of different castes can still cause family conflicts.

Upriver can be found the Fulani, many of whom have now settled and become

These Serahuli men discuss village affairs in the cool of a thatched shelter. It is the women who will be working in the vegetable gardens, growing food for the family.

farmers. Different groups speak different Fulani dialects. Most Aku, descendants of the freed slaves, speak English and live in Banjul, as do the Jola (JOE-lah) people, who have migrated to Gambia from Senegal looking for work (see SENEGAL).

Islam arrived in western Africa more than one thousand years ago, and many peoples adopted the Islamic faith. Today 90 percent of the people of Gambia are Muslim, and daily prayer is an integral part of their everyday life.

The Europeans introduced Christianity to the region, but their missionaries had little success. The religion they offered was regarded as the religion of invaders. Today there are a small number of Christians, mostly among the Aku people in Banjul, where there is a small Anglican cathedral. In the remoter parts of the country, people practice their traditional beliefs in the power of spirits.

Elementary education in Gambia is free but not compulsory. Only about one-third of elementary-age children go to school. Poor families keep children at home to help on the farm and in the house. The country is too small to support a university, so

197

Vessels of every size use the Gambia River to bring goods from the coast to the interior. Many small ferries, as seen here, carry people between the northern and southern banks.

Gambians who seek a university education go to Sierra Leone, Great Britain, or the United States.

Although there are several general hospitals, health centers, and maternity and child-care clinics, there are few trained medical personnel to provide quality health care for the rapidly expanding population. Diseases such as dysentery, malaria, and tuberculosis are widespread. The surgical procedure of female genital cutting is very common (see SOMALIA).

The main route for transporting people and freight is the Gambia River. It is navigable for about 200 miles (320 kilometers). Several ferries also make regular north-south crossings. An all-weather road follows the same route as the river. Banjul is the chief port, where large vessels anchor at sea and small boats carry their goods to land.

Most Gambians are subsistence farmers, keeping a few animals and growing crops such as cassava, yams, rice, sorghum, and millet. The main cash crop is peanuts, with production steadily increasing as better fertilizers and seeds are more widely used. To avoid too great a dependence on this one crop, the government is encouraging rice, cotton, sisal, fruit, and tobacco production. It is also trying to help the fishing industry by lending money for motorized boats and huts to smoke the fish for export.

Less than 5 percent of all Gambians work in the small-scale industries that mostly process peanuts, fish, and hides. Tourism is important to the Gambian economy, with Europeans coming to enjoy the sunshine and beaches of the coastal resorts.

Life of the People

The low-lying town of Banjul is small. Many people living there work for the government, and a few are employed in small industrial firms. Buying and selling, however small scale, is the way most people survive. Albert Market has been the lively center of town life since the 1800s.

The sea dominates the lives of coastal Gambians. Each community has its strip of beach and its canoes. Every day the village canoes take to the sea, returning with a great variety of fish.

Along the river, people live in small communities, each with its own walled vegetable garden. The men work in the fields, growing the cash crops, particularly peanuts. The women grow food for the family—onions, radishes, oranges, bananas, cassavas, yams. Whatever they have left, they sell from small stalls at the roadside.

The different peoples of Gambia tend to have different food specialties. The Wolof enjoy *benachin* (BEH-nah-shihn), a stew made with meat or fish and served with rice and vegetables. The Malinke are particularly good at making *domoda* (doe-MOE-dah), which is a stew made with peanuts, okra, tomatoes, and onions. For the Aku, red palm-oil stew made with smoked fish and green vegetables is a favorite dish. When out and about in the towns, people buy a great variety of snacks, or "small chop." Some of these are pastry fritters, fish cakes, and roasted peanuts.

Palm wine remains a popular drink.

When they have free time, many Gambians love to play and watch soccer. They are also avid swimmers. A long established and popular sport is wrestling; matches take place on weekend afternoons in most villages. The wrestlers wear brightly colored loincloths with a fake animal tail attached, and their arms are covered in charms. Their supporters encourage them with drums and whistles and the chants of cheerleaders.

Among the crafts practiced in Gambia are wood carving, jewelry making, and batik cloth printing and weaving. Musical instruments are also made, particularly the *kora* (KOE-rah), a stringed instrument traditionally used by musicians called *griots* (GREE-oes). In the past, noble Wolof families employed griots to tell stories and sing the praises of their employers.

Complicated rhythms played on different kinds of drums provide the music for these dancers. The women wear traditional clothes—skirts, blouses, and head ties.

GHANA

GHANA IS A COUNTRY ON THE WESTERN COAST OF AFRICA. Part of its land lies under the waters of Lake Volta, the world's largest artificial lake.

Ghana is bordered on the south by the Atlantic Ocean. Strong surf pounds the coast, and there are no natural harbors.

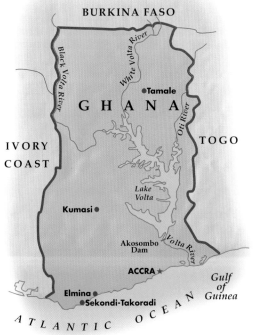

Mountains run along Ghana's eastern borders. Marshy plains lie close to the southern coast. The low-lying Volta River Basin divides the central uplands. Low, rolling plateaus cover the west and north. Vegetation varies from dense rain forest in the south to savanna grassland in the north-central regions and dry, dusty plains in the far north.

CLIMATE

Ghana has a hot, tropical climate. Temperatures remain about the same year-round. The north has a single rainy season from June to October. The humid southern and central regions have two rainy seasons, from March to June and September to October. The area around Accra is drier than the coastal lands farther west.

Average January temperature: *79°F (26°C)*

Average July temperature: *84°F (29°C)*

Average annual precipitation:
   in the southwest: *82 in. (208 cm)*
   in the north: *39 in. (99 cm)*

Crowds of people shop at one of the main markets in Accra, the biggest, liveliest city in Ghana. All kinds of goods, from fresh fruits to brightly colored cloth, are on sale here.

The Ashanti Kingdom

Precise details about the early history of Ghana (GAH-nuh) are not yet known. The earliest evidence of settlement yet discovered was found along the coast and dates from around 40,000 B.C.E. Archaeologists also believe that peoples with a knowledge of farming lived in the Ghana region by around 600 B.C.E. By around 100 C.E. ironworking techniques were known. The gold fields of central Ghana were being worked by people who traded with the powerful city of Djenné (je-NAE), in present-day Mali, by around 1400 C.E. The Ewe (EH-vae) people arrived in the region from the east in about 1450 and settled along the coast.

The most powerful people in Ghana from the 1400s to the 1800s were the Ashanti (uh-SHAN-tee), who had migrated to Ghana from the savanna lands to the north. They settled in the central region around 1000 C.E., cleared farms from the rain forest, and began to mine gold. Several small states emerged, ruled by independent chiefs. During the 1670s Chief Osei Tutu joined all these small states together and proclaimed himself *asantehene* (uh-sahn-tuh-HAE-nee), Ashanti king. He founded a new capital city at Kumasi (koo-MAH-see), a site chosen for him by a powerful priest. Legends tell how the priest then called down a golden stool from heaven as a royal throne for the asantehene and a symbol of the Ashanti people's soul.

Over the next one hundred years, the Ashanti people grew more powerful by conquering many smaller states in Ghana

FACTS AND FIGURES

Official name: *Republic of Ghana*

Status: *Independent state*

Capital: *Accra*

Major towns: *Kumasi, Tamale, Sekondi-Takoradi*

Area: *92,100 square miles (238,539 square kilometers)*

Population: *19,700,000*

Population density: *214 per square mile (83 per square kilometer)*

Peoples: *44 percent Akan (Ashanti and Fante); 16 percent Mole-Dagbani; 13 percent Ewe; 8 percent Ga-Adangme; many smaller groups*

Official language: *English*

Currency: *Cedi*

National days: *Fourth Republic Day (January 7); Independence Day (March 6); Revolution Day (June 4); Republic Day (July 1); Farmers' Day (December 2); Anniversary of the Second Revolution (December 31)*

Country's name: *After independence in 1960, the country's rulers took the name from the ancient kingdom called Ghana, which, from around 700 to 1100 C.E., ruled a rich empire in part of present-day Mali and Mauritania.*

and neighboring Ivory Coast (see IVORY COAST). Conquered peoples had to send taxes and laborers to Kumasi. To cope with this larger kingdom, Ashanti kings employed many chiefs and royal officials to help them rule.

The Ashanti peoples' wealth came mainly from trade, though they were extremely

Time line:	Earliest evidence of human habitation along the coast	Akan people arrive in the region	Ewe people arrive	Portuguese begin to build slave forts
	ca. 40,000 B.C.E.	ca. 1000 C.E.	ca. 1450	1482

Royal Capital

At the heart of Kumasi stands the Asantehene (king's) Palace. Many wonderful Ashanti royal treasures, made of pure gold, are displayed in the museum nearby. The Ashanti king still lives in Kumasi and appears in public to receive homage from his subjects at the Adae Festival, held twice every forty-two days, the length of the Ashanti month.

Visitors also come to Kumasi to see the Okomfo Anokye Sword. It stands half in and half out of the ground. According to legend, it marks the spot where the Ashanti's sacred golden stool came down to Earth from the sky. Other legends warn that if anyone ever pulls the sword out of the ground, the Ashanti kingdom will disappear.

skilled artisans as well. Precious Ashanti gold was carried northward across the Sahara to sell in cities in Egypt and the Middle East. It was also sent southward to fetch high prices at European trading stations on the Ghana coast.

The Ashanti kings never managed to conquer a group of small states in the north and northeast of present-day Ghana and across the borders in Togo and Burkina Faso. The people living there spoke varieties of the Mole and More languages, such as Mamprusi and Dagomba, and owed loyalty to the powerful Mossi kings of Burkina Faso (see BURKINA FASO). In

1962 archaeologists found the remains of the Dagomba royal capital close to the city of Tamale (tah-MAH-lae) in Ghana's northern region.

Slave Traders and Gold Seekers

During the 1400s Portuguese slave traders and gold seekers explored the west African coast. By 1482 they had built their first fort in Ghana. Soon afterward a whole chain of forts were built along the coast.

Over the next three centuries, the selling of humans became a thriving industry. Ashanti chiefs, who already used slave labor to work their gold fields, profited from the slave trade by selling slaves that had been captured in war to the Portuguese. The chiefs also had contacts with African slave dealers in inland regions. During the early seventeenth century, the Portuguese slave traders started to ship large numbers of Ghanaian people to the Americas to work on plantations.

In 1642 the Dutch conquered the Portuguese forts and took control of the slave trade. The Dutch also purchased gold from Ghanaian mine owners. The British became rivals of the Dutch, and by the nineteenth century the British controlled most of coastal Ghana. In 1807 the British abolished the slave commerce and began to exploit other trade items—palm oil, cocoa, rubber, gold, and timber.

Between 1807 and 1814 the Ashanti launched a series of invasions of land occupied by the Fante (FAHN-tee). A combined British and Fante force defeated

Era of slave trading	Dutch conquer Portuguese forts	Ashanti kingdom founded	Ashanti kingdom expands to cover most of modern Ghana	Southern Ghana becomes a British colony
ca. 1500–1807	1642	1670s	1717–1750	1874

Fishing boats and a passenger ferry at Elmina (el-MEE-nuh) on Ghana's southwest coast. In the background is Saint George's Fort, built by Portuguese slave traders in 1482.

the Ashanti in 1826. The British government declared a strip of land along the coast to be under British protection and sent British troops to guard it.

However, throughout the rest of the nineteenth century, the Ashanti fought fiercely against the British. In 1890 the regions where the Ewe people lived were divided between the Gold Coast and German-ruled Togoland (see TOGO). The British finally took control of both the coastal and inland regions in 1901, and the following year Ghana was declared a British colony called the Gold Coast.

The British supervised the mining of gold, bauxite, manganese, and diamonds and planted vast cocoa plantations.

Nkrumah and Independence

From the beginning of British rule, Ghanaians campaigned for self-government, but Ghana did not finally win independence until 1957. Kwame Nkrumah became the first prime minister and later its president. Although multiparty elections had brought him to power, Nkrumah revised the constitution in 1964 to make Ghana a one-party state. An ambitious leader, Nkrumah planned many grand projects, such as the Akosombo Dam, which created Lake Volta,

Eastern boundary decided in treaty with Germany, splitting Ewe people in two	End of Ashanti fight against Great Britain	Whole region becomes a British colony, the Gold Coast	Ghana becomes independent; Kwame Nkrumah is prime minister
1890	**1901**	**1902**	**1957**

the largest artificial lake in the world. These projects almost bankrupted the country, and in 1966 he was overthrown.

Rawlings in Power

Nkrumah was followed by a series of military and civilian governments. Some were corrupt, others simply inefficient. Their policies caused tremendous economic problems and social hardship. The last army council was overturned by Flight Lieutenant Jerry Rawlings in 1979. He aimed to end corruption and renew national pride. He allowed democratic elections that were already planned to be held. Hilla Limann was elected president, but Rawlings staged another coup in December 1981 and replaced Limann as government leader.

At first many army officers, businesspeople, and well-educated civilians distrusted Rawlings, and there were more attempted coups. Rawlings stayed in power, however, and pushed forward his plans to reform the government and rebuild the economy. He sought advice and aid from international organizations, such as the International Monetary Fund, and encouraged independent businesses to take over state-run industries, which were nearing collapse. His government paid cocoa farmers fairer prices for their crops and

President Jerry Rawlings talking with Ghanaian children at a rally. Rawlings has been the most important politician in Ghana for the last twenty years.

fostered cocoa replanting programs on abandoned farms and fields. The government also planned large projects to improve Ghana's roads, ports, and water and power supplies. By 1990 the government realized it was time to return to democratic rule. It introduced a new multiparty constitution and free multiparty elections in 1992. Rawlings ran for president as a civilian politician and won; he was reelected for a second four-year term in 1996.

Today Ghana's economy is still making progress, though a sudden drop in world gold or cocoa prices would cause serious problems, since these commodities create much of the country's wealth. However, compared with many other west African nations, Ghana's prospects look good.

Nkrumah overthrown by army	Elections and civilian rule	Jerry Rawlings seizes power; reforms government and economy	Multiparty elections; Rawlings returned to power	Rawlings reelected
1966	**1979**	**1981**	**1992**	**1996**

The Peoples of Ghana

Although Ghana is not a particularly large country, it is home to a great many different peoples. The Akan (uh-KAHN) peoples form the largest group in the population; they include the Ashanti, who live in the central region, and the Fante, who live near the coast. The Ashanti can also be found in Ivory Coast and Togo. The Mole-Dagbani (MOEL duhg-BAH-nee) peoples and their neighbors, the Gonja (GAWN-jah) and the Dagomba (duh-GOEM-bah), live in the north of Ghana as farmers and herders. They speak Mole languages and are related to the More-speaking Mossi (MOE-see) people of Burkina Faso (see BURKINA FASO). The Ga-Adangme (GAH-dahng-mae) peoples fish and farm on the coast near the Volta Delta in the south and speak Ga languages. The Ewe live in the south and east and speak Ewe; some Ewe also live in Togo (see

This girl from the Dagomba people of northern Ghana is about twelve years old. The tattoos on her forehead and at the corners of her mouth are a sign of beauty.

TOGO). Traditionally the Ewe were organized into many small kingdoms, each ruled by a council of chiefs. Even today there are over one hundred Ewe groups.

All these separate groups share a strong sense of pride in being Ghanaian. This feeling of nationalism developed during the struggle for independence and in the years afterward.

There are also over 100,000 refugees living in Ghana, displaced from their homes by wars in nearby Liberia and Togo (see LIBERIA and TOGO).

Because there are so many different peoples in Ghana, there are almost one hundred different languages and local dialects. Most Ghanaian people speak at least two, and often three, languages: their native dialect, one of the majority group languages (Akan, Ewe, Ga, or Mole), and English.

Families and Clans

All Ghanaian people belong to large extended families, comprising a husband, his wife or wives, their children, and a network of close relatives, such as grandparents, nephews, or cousins, who depend on them to survive. All family members are expected to help and support one another and share their wealth. Traditionally Ghanaian men had more than one wife if they could afford to. This custom, called polygamy, is still continued by some wealthy men today.

Among the Akan peoples, families are organized along maternal lines; family members trace their descent from women, not men. Husbands and wives each live in separate homes, usually with their mother, if she is still alive. Wives visit their husbands to bring them meals and spend time in their company. They inherit property (houses and fields) from their

Babies are welcomed into Ghanaian families, and traditional customs celebrate their birth. This baby's head is being shaved as part of a name-giving ceremony.

live in towns tend to have smaller families.

Most women today still work at their long-established tasks, growing food and selling fish or farm produce. In towns and cities a large number of women work as market traders. Many educated women also work as nurses, teachers, and civil servants.

Although a number of Ghanaians live in big cities

mothers and pass it on to their children. Most other Ghanaian peoples, including the Ewe, inherit land and trace their descent from men, but husbands and wives still sometimes live in separate homes.

Clans are groups of families who trace their descent from one ancestor. All Ghanaians recognize the importance of clan relationships, but clans are most powerful among the Akan. Each clan is headed by elders and a chief. In the past they were very powerful; though today's chiefs have less influence, they are still respected. They may be consulted by the government as representatives of the community or play an important part in local politics.

Traditionally, women's most important task was to produce children. Many Ghanaian people believed that past family members are reborn in new babies. Today many Ghanaian women still feel this way and like to have five or more children; college-educated, professional women who

Names and Days

Akan (Ashanti and Fante) people are named after the day of the week on which they were born.

Girls' names:

Monday: Ajoa (AHJ-wah)
Tuesday: Aba (AH-bah) or Abena (uh-BAE-nah)
Wednesday: Akua (AH-kwah)
Thursday: Yaa (YAH)
Friday: Efua (eh-FWEE-ah)
Saturday: Ama (AH-mah)
Sunday: Esi (AE-see)

Boys' names:

Monday: Kojo (KOE-joe)
Tuesday: Kobina (koe-BEE-nah) or Kwabena (KWAH-bae-nah)
Wednesday: Kweku (KWAE-koo)
Thursday: Ekow (ih-KOE) or Yao (YAH-oe)
Friday: Kofi (KOE-fee)
Saturday: Kwame (KWAH-mee) or Kwamena (kwah-MAE-nah)
Sunday: Kwesi (KWAE-see)

The Yam Festival

The Odwira Festival is the most important yearly celebration among the Ashanti people. It is held in autumn, the time when new yams are ready. They cannot be eaten until the second day of the festival, when they are paraded through the streets.

The whole festival lasts for five days and is celebrated slightly differently in each community. Throughout the festival, music and drumming abound. On the first day the path leading toward the chiefs' burial chambers is cleaned. On the second day priests make offerings at the burial chambers and a great yam parade takes place. On the third day people mourn and fast. On the fourth a splendid feast for everyone in the community is held at the local chief's house. That night, everyone must stay indoors, to avoid catching sight of the chiefs' thrones, symbols of the dead men's spirits, which are carried to the river to be ceremonially washed. On the fifth and final day, chiefs and other important clan members, dressed in their best, parade through the town in a grand procession to pay homage to the senior local chief. Some are carried shoulder high on litters and shaded with brilliantly colored umbrellas. Then people play music and dance late into the night.

and work in modern offices, stores, and factories, they still maintain links with their families and home villages. Big cities are multiethnic; people from different regions live and work side by side. They also like to belong to social clubs and other organizations in which they meet people who come from the same villages, speak the same language, and share the same background.

Religions and Festivals

Ghana's religious beliefs are a mixture of old and new. About 40 percent of the population follows traditional African beliefs, 30 percent are Muslim, and 20 percent are Christian. There are also many newer religious groups that combine Christian beliefs with African ones. Followers of African religions honor their ancestors with ceremonies and offerings.

An Ashanti chief is carried through the streets of the town of Akrokeri in a yam festival procession. Giant umbrellas and gilded swords are signs of royal rank.

Harvesting cocoa pods at a plantation in southern Ghana. Each pod contains many cocoa beans, which are washed, dried, ground, and mixed with sugar to make chocolate.

evil forces that can harm individuals or whole communities.

Ghanaian people enjoy celebrating festivals, most of which have a religious origin. Other festivals celebrate harvest time or commemorate famous events that happened long ago. There are dozens of festivals in Ghana, held in different places throughout the year. Many include spectacular dancing and drumming.

Earning a Living

Over half of Ghana's population survives by farming, working on their own plots of land or on big cocoa and banana plantations owned by large companies. Different crops are grown in different regions. Coconuts are one of the few crops grown along the coast. They are a source of food for both humans and livestock. Most coastal people live by fishing and by making salt from seawater. A little farther inland and in the swampy Volta River Delta, farmers grow corn, vegetables, cassava, and cocoa in plots cleared from the rain forests.

Ancestors are important because they protect the clan; though present everywhere, they cannot be seen. Followers of African religions and the newer groups believe that their priests have powers as healers and fortune-tellers. Priests use fetishes (charms) to drive away

In the central uplands cocoa is the main crop, but women also raise vegetables in garden plots to feed their families, and hunters shoot wild animals in the forests. The Volta Basin is dry, with badly eroded soil. Few crops grow well here, but women gather nuts from shea trees. Oil from these nuts is exported and used to make high-quality soaps and cosmetics. On eastern mountain slopes, close to the Togo border, farmers grow rice, sweet potatoes, yams, and coffee. In the dry, dusty north they grow millet and keep cattle.

Ghana contains rich reserves of gold as well as industrial-grade diamonds, bauxite (used to make aluminum), and manganese. Its rain forests contain valuable timber. All these bring Ghana considerable wealth. Ghanaian peoples' average income is twice that of inhabitants of most other African nations south of the Sahara, but there is a high price to pay in environmental terms. Gold mining, in particular, causes serious pollution in rivers and streams, poisoning drinking water and killing fish. Logging is quickly destroying many rain forests.

Corn, Millet, Soup, and Sauces

Staple foods vary from region to region. In the south they include *kenkey* (KEHN-kee), which is fermented corn flour wrapped in corn leaves and steamed; it's eaten with pepper and onion sauce and fried fish. In the north, *tozafi* (toh-ZAH-fee), or boiled millet, is more popular. Tozafi is eaten with soups made from palm-nuts or okra-seed

Chicken and Bean Soup

You will need:

  2 large or 3 small pieces of chicken
  1 large chopped onion
  1 chopped green pepper
  4 1/4 cups (1 liter) water
  salt
  pepper
  1 pinch chili pepper

Mix all the ingredients in a large saucepan, cover with lid, and simmer until chicken is cooked (about forty-five minutes).

Remove chicken meat from the bones, cut into bite-sized pieces, and return meat to soup. Throw bones away.

Add:

  8 oz (225 g) of cooked haricot beans or cowpeas
  1 lb (450 g) of tomatoes, chopped
  1 small eggplant, cut into cubes
  10 okra pods, washed and trimmed (optional)

Add more water if necessary (the soup should be thick but not solid). Simmer gently for another thirty minutes or until the eggplant and okra are cooked.

This quantity serves four people.

These people are using a hand-powered mill to grind corn kernels to make flour. It's hard work but easier than the traditional method of pounding corn with a heavy log.

pods. Various other starchy foods—cassavas, yams, and sweet potatoes—are also cooked and served with strong-tasting sauces. Favorite foods also include plantains, beans, pumpkin seeds, pineapples, coconuts, and peanuts, which are chopped and used to make sauces.

Fish and seafood are sold at markets close to the coast; in forest regions farther inland, people eat guinea fowls, grasscutters (rats), lizards, cats, and dogs. Good-quality chocolate is made from locally grown cocoa, but some Ghanaians prefer *kelewele* (keh-leh-WAE-lae), which are hot, sweet plantain chips, spiced with ginger. *Krakro* (KRAH-kroe), which are fried cakes made from sweet potatoes, are also popular. European-style beer; cola; fruit drinks; *askenkee* (AHS-kehn-kai), which is a cool drink made from corn flour and water; and *pito* (PEE-toe), or millet beer, are all refreshing drinks. Palm liquor is fiery and strong, and palm wine is widely drank in the south.

Homes, New and Old

About one-third of the population lives in towns and cities; two-thirds in the countryside. Accra (AH-kruh), the capital, is home to about one-tenth of the country's population. It is one of Africa's biggest cities. Many people in Accra live in crowded concrete apartment buildings that were built shortly after independence and are now in need of repair. In some parts of the city stand modern office buildings, hotels, nightclubs, and expensive shops; in other parts open drains and sewers can still cause health problems.

Along the coast the Fante live in fishing villages built of wood, mud, and thatch. Inland the Ashanti live in hillside villages in forest or cocoa-plantation clearings. Traditionally, Ashanti homes are built as a cluster of separate chambers around a

Young village children gather outside the thatched house belonging to their chief's senior wife to listen to her stories and sing traditional songs.

walled courtyard, which acts as an outdoor room. Walls used to be made of wood and plaster and were often decorated with elaborate raised patterns. Nowadays concrete and grooved iron are sometimes used instead. Similar round straw-roofed houses are built in the north; they are typically painted yellow and have brown designs.

Health and Education

Ghana's hot, moist climate means that it can be an unhealthy place to live. Many killer infections flourish, including cholera, yellow fever, hepatitis, dysentery, and polio. There are also dangerous diseases caused by parasites, including malaria (carried by mosquitoes) and schistosomiasis (carried by water snails). River blindness (onchocerciasis) affects many people living on the shores of Lake Volta. Ghana has a large number of people, especially women and children, with HIV and AIDS. Life

This traditional healer displays many different medicines and fetishes (charms) in his stall, including porcupine quills, tortoiseshell, tree bark, herbs, spices, and seashells.

Saving Sight

River blindness (onchocerciasis) affects millions of people in western Africa. It is spread by blackflies, which bite humans and pass on tiny worms. These breed in the human bloodstream and migrate to the eyes, where they cause cloudy vision and eventually blindness. Until recently, this disease ruined the lives of many Ghanaians who lived beside water where blackflies swarmed. The World Health Organization has run a massive campaign to destroy the flies in Ghana and nearby nations. The campaign has been a great success. Now villages by the river are safer places to live.

expectancy is about fifty-four years for men and fifty-eight years for women.

Hospital beds and trained doctors are in short supply; most can be found only in towns and cities, which are out of reach to two-thirds of the population. People living far from towns often rely on traditional priests and herbalists for medical help. However, the government has recently introduced a basic health care program for the countryside. It has also made plans to provide clean drinking water in many remote areas.

Literacy levels are high in Ghana; over three-quarters of all men and over half of

Crafts for Kings

Brilliantly colored kente *(KEHN-tee) cloth has a long history. It was originally made for Ashanti rulers but is now worn on special occasions by people rich enough to afford it. It is woven in narrow strips, each with a complicated pattern. The strips are then carefully joined together to make a long, loose robe. The best-quality kente cloth has a special name,* adweneasa *(ahd-weh-nee-AH-sah), which means "the weaver's skill is exhausted."*

Ghanaian artisans are also famous for their fine wood carving, leather work, and woven baskets. Ewe men carve beautiful wooden figures of gods and spirits and also statues of children, which are buried alongside childless women.

For many years, Ghana was known as "the Gold Coast," partly because of the gold found in its rocks and streams, and also because of its wonderfully skilled gold

Examples of brightly colored Kente cloth. Kente cloth always has patterns of stripes and squares. It is usually woven from cotton; the finest is made of silk.

workers. Ashanti goldsmiths were especially famous; they made gold jewelry and regalia for their kings, including the sacred Gold Stool, a symbol of Ashanti power. Beautiful gold jewelry is still made in Ghana today.

These finely decorated gold disks were worn as badges of office by senior officials at the court of the Ashanti kings of Ghana over one hundred years ago.

212

all women can read and write. Education is provided by the state, but even the poorest children have to pay for their schoolbooks. There are three stages in schooling: elementary school (six years), junior secondary school (three years), and senior secondary school (three years). Most children attend elementary and then junior secondary schools until they are about fifteen. A few families do not send their daughters to school at all. They claim that girls are needed to help in the fields or around the home. There are four universities and many colleges and polytechnic institutes.

Music and Dance

In the past the best musicians played to entertain chiefs and their visitors. Their style of music is still played today, but now it is available for everyone to hear. The most popular traditional instruments are drums, horns, and xylophones. Dagomba drummers are especially skillful. Many long-established songs and dances are still performed at religious festivals, and the Ewe people are famous for their dance music and work songs.

In the 1950s and 1960s, modern Ghanaian popular music—known as highlife—became famous in dance halls and nightclubs throughout Africa and beyond. It mixed African rhythms and tunes with many different kinds of Western music, from brass bands to missionary hymns. During the 1980s and 1990s, Ghanaian bands experimented with many of the latest styles in pop and rock.

Ashanti musicians blowing horns made from elephant tusks. Similar horns were played at Ashanti royal courts, along with big drums, during important ceremonies.

GUINEA

GUINEA LIES IN THE FAR WEST OF AFRICA, bordering the Atlantic Ocean in the southwest.

Guinea is full of contrasts. Within its boundaries are low-lying coastal lagoons, rolling savanna grasslands, beautiful mountain scenery, and magnificent tropical rain forests.

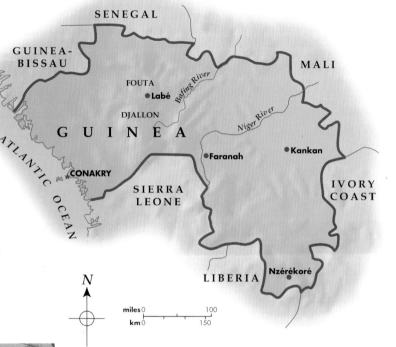

CLIMATE

One of the wettest countries in Africa, Guinea has a hot, tropical climate. Temperatures remain about the same year-round. The rainy season lasts from April to November, with peak rainfall in July and August. The marshy western coastline receives the most rain; the high mountains in the Fouta Djallon district receive the least. In northern regions a hot, dry wind called the harmattan sometimes blows from December to March.

Average January temperature: *79°F (26°C)*
Average July temperature: *79°F (26°C)*
Average annual precipitation:
   coast: *170 in. (432 cm)*
   eastern mountains: *63 in. (160 cm)*

These villagers are building a new well to provide clean drinking water for their families. Community action like this is vital for Guinea's future.

214

Guinea's Past

Guinea (GIH-nee) is a fairly new nation; its boundaries were not fixed until it became part of the French colonial empire around 1900 C.E. For centuries before, the many different peoples who lived in Guinea shared a hand in creating several powerful civilizations that flourished in western Africa.

From around 700 C.E., Malinke (muh-LIHN-keh) and Susu (SOO-soo) peoples moved into the area. They cleared rain forest land and worked as farmers. From 900 to 1100, Guinea was ruled by the empire of Ghana, based in present-day Mauritania and Mali (see MALI). From 1100 to 1450, it became part of the Mali Empire. Then, from around 1450 to 1600, it was ruled by Mali's successor, Songhai (see MALI). All these empires had boundaries that stretched far wider than present-day Guinea. All were rich from collecting taxes from merchants who traveled across the Sahara between western Africa and the Mediterranean coast, and all built fine towns with colleges and mosques. Much of Ghana's and Mali's wealth originated in Guinea's Bambuk and Buré gold fields.

The original inhabitants of Fouta Djallon (FOO-tah jah-LONE), a mountainous district in western Guinea, were Fulani (foo-LAH-nee) farmers. Around 1200, another group of Fulani began to settle in the Fouta Djallon region. They were cattle herders from the north, who brought the religion of Islam with them, and by 1750 they had established a powerful Muslim kingdom in Fouta Djallon. They waged

FACTS AND FIGURES

Official name: *République de Guinée*

Status: *Independent state*

Capital: *Conakry*

Major towns: *Kankan, Labé, Nzérékoré*

Area: *94,925 square miles (245,856 square kilometers)*

Population: *7,500,000*

Population density: *79 per square mile (31 per square kilometer)*

Peoples: *39 percent Fulani; 23 percent Malinke; 11 percent Susu; 6 percent Kissi; 5 percent Kpelle; and many other groups*

Official language: *French*

Currency: *Guinea franc*

National days: *Market Women's Revolt (August 27); Independence Day (October 1); Armed Forces Day (November 1)*

Country's name: *Guinea was the European name for a large part of the western coast of Africa. It may be derived from Djenné, the old trading center, now in Mali, or from the Ghana empire, or it may come from the berber word aguinaw, meaning "black man."*

holy war against their neighbors, selling those they had captured into slavery or keeping them as their own slaves. By about 1800 two of their provinces, Labé and Timbo, had become virtually independent, controlling all the land in northern and northwestern Guinea.

During the nineteenth century the French and British competed over control of Guinea. The French defeated the British but were strongly opposed by armies led

Time line:	Malinke and Susu people arrive	Guinea is part of Ghana Empire	Guinea is part of Mali Empire	Guinea is part of Songhai Empire
	ca. 700 C.E.	ca. 900–1100	ca. 1100–1450	ca. 1450–1600

An illustration from a French magazine reports the capture of Malinke leader Samori Touré by a French army officer in 1898. Touré fought French colonial rule for fifteen years.

by Samori Touré, a Malinke leader, who conquered surrounding states to build a powerful trading empire southeast of Fouta Djallon in the 1860s and 1870s. Samori Touré's iron foundries manufactured and repaired guns, enabling his armies to provide the strongest opposition the French faced in all of western Africa. Samori Touré was finally captured and deported in 1898. The Kissi (KIH-see) people living in the forests tried to fight, but they had no central organization and, village by village, they surrendered.

In 1895 Guinea became part of French West Africa. French settlers set up rubber plantations, cultivated coffee and bananas for export, and mined bauxite. French people ruled Guinea mainly for their own benefit and did not provide education or welfare services for the local people.

After 1945 a powerful nationalist movement emerged in Guinea, led by Ahmed Sekou Touré, a communist trade-union leader with links to similar movements in other French West African countries. He led strikes to demand higher wages and reform of labor laws.

A Move toward Independence

Sekou Touré became mayor of Conakry (KAH-nuh-kree) in 1955 and chief minister of Guinea, though still owing obedience to France, in 1957. He campaigned vigorously for independence. The French offered a referendum to Guinea and other French countries in western Africa. Guineans were able to vote on whether or not they wished to continue links with France. Sekou Touré organized a successful campaign to persuade people to vote no to France. Guinea was the only colony to reject French proposals to turn African colonies into semi-independent members of a French commonwealth.

Guinea was declared independent from France in 1958. France withdrew all aid, administrators, technicians, and equipment (even office furniture and telephones) in a deliberate attempt to bankrupt the new

Fulani people establish powerful kingdom in Fouta Djallon	France defeats Great Britain for control of Guinea; Malinke leader Samori Touré fights against the French	France makes Guinea part of colony of French West Africa	Guineans demand independence from France
1720s–1740s	**1870s–1890s**	**1895**	**1940s–1950s**

state; the French wanted to frighten their other colonies into staying with France. Sekou Touré sought help from the former Soviet Union (USSR) and planned a communist-style, state-run economy and society.

However, the French boycott ruined the country. Guinea became very poor, and serious food shortages plagued the country. People protested, but Sekou Touré punished opponents severely. In 1967 he introduced strict new laws against anyone who criticized him, setting up revolutionary committees throughout the country, recruiting a network of security police and spies, and imprisoning anyone he suspected of opposing him. He aimed to destroy the traditional independence of the Fulani people; the Fulani leader was starved to death in prison. Many Guineans fled to other countries to escape. Foreign visitors were kept out, the media was censored, and Guinea became increasingly cut off from the outside world.

In 1970 Guinean exiles, soldiers from neighboring Guinea-Bissau, and Portuguese officers led an unsuccessful invasion. They hoped to destroy camps belonging to Guinea-Bissau rebels who were hiding in Guinea. After this, Sekou Touré became even more suspicious about plots against him, and there were more human rights abuses. Meanwhile, the economic crisis

President Sekou Touré visiting communist leader Nikita Khruschev in Moscow, capital of the USSR, in 1960. For many years Sekou Touré relied on the USSR for support.

deepened, and drought killed crops and livestock in the northern regions.

By 1977 food prices had spiraled out of control. Market women in Conakry rioted. Protests spread throughout Guinea, and Sekou Touré was forced to promise economic reforms. He began to seek support and aid from right-wing regimes. The army lost confidence in him and planned a coup, but Sekou Touré died in 1984 before the army could remove him from power.

Supported by the army, Colonel Lansana Conté became head of the new government. Conté introduced political freedoms and

Independence; Ahmed Sekou Touré becomes president, plans communist state	Sekou Touré terrorizes opponents; many Guineans go into exile	Riots; Sekou Touré abandons communist policies	Sekou Touré dies; Lansana Conté becomes president; frees political prisoners
1958	**1967–1977**	**1977**	**1984**

economic reforms designed to end state control of business and encourage private enterprise. He sought aid from friendly governments and advice from foreign loan-giving organizations, such as the International Monetary Fund. The strict economic policies they demanded in return for financial help led to more price increases and riots. In 1992 aid-giving governments encouraged Conté to introduce multiparty democracy, freedom of the press, and open political debate. Today there are over forty new political parties.

The first free elections were held in 1993. Conté and his supporters won power but were accused of cheating. Over the following three years, the army tried, but failed, to seize power three times. After more disputed elections in December 1998, Conté remained in power.

People, Languages, Faiths

Guinea is home to many different peoples. Guineans speak different languages, follow different customs, and make their living in many different ways. Guinea has a culture that is based on storytelling, music, and dance, and a rich heritage of ancient traditions.

There are three main ethnic/language groups—the Fulani, the Malinke, and the Susu—and almost thirty smaller ones. They inhabit different regions of the country; the Susu live as farmers along the coast, while the Malinke survive by herding cattle on the savanna plains. The Fulani live in the Fouta Djallon Mountains; they

Men and women work together to build a new village home. It is fashioned with traditional materials—sun-dried mud brick, wooden rafters, and thick grass thatch.

Conté ends state control of economy and encourages private enterprise	Multiparty democracy introduced	Conté elected president in multiparty election	Conté reelected president
1985	**1992**	**1993**	**1998**

Until recently, about two million Guineans lived and worked abroad. They left Guinea to escape economic hardship and persecution by Sekou Touré. Today some of them are returning to their homes and families. There are also at least 650,000 refugees living in camps in southern Guinea, escaping from civil wars in Liberia and Sierra Leone (see LIBERIA and SIERRA LEONE).

Guinea's official language is French, introduced when large parts of western Africa were ruled by France. But it is not spoken by most

Few everyday people in Guinea speak French at home, but they need it to get top jobs. Young people learn French in high schools and in colleges and universities.

also keep cattle and grow crops. Other peoples, such as the Kissi, the Kpelle (kuh-PEH-lee), the Loma (LOE-mah), and the Koma (KOE-mah), live in the rain forests, where they hunt wild animals and grow vegetables in forest clearings.

Since independence in 1958 tensions have sometimes arisen between the different peoples, mostly for political reasons. Sekou Touré was a Malinke; he distrusted the Fulani and treated them very badly. By the time he died, he was hated and feared by many Guineans. As a result, few Malinke have since been offered jobs with power. The second president, Lansana Conté, and most of the powerful people in Guinea today are Susu. The Fulani, who had their own independent state before the French arrived, resent their continued exclusion from political power.

Pomdo *Statues*

The Kissi people live in southeastern Guinea. They are expert farmers who specialize in growing rice. The Kissi honor their ancestors, believing that the ancestors bless them and help their crops to grow. They also honor small stone statues called pomdo *(PAWM-doe), which are often found buried in the soil of their fields. Occasionally they are found in the forest. The Kissi believe that the statues embody ancestors who lived in their lands long ago.*

All the pomdo statues are several hundred years old. Their origins are a mystery. Archaeologists think that they must have been created by people living in southern Guinea some time before 1300 C.E.

219

Since jobs in Guinea can be hard to find, some women go to college to learn useful skills, such as needlework, that will help them earn money.

ordinary people; they speak their own languages, mainly Fulani, Malinke, and Susu. Businesspeople and traders, who need to speak with buyers and sellers from all the different regions, use a special language called Dyula (JOO-lah), the common language of trade in the days of the Mali and Songhai Empires. Arabic is the holy language used for prayer by many Muslim people. Almost 85 percent of Guineans are Muslim; about 8 percent are Christian, and about 7 percent follow traditional local beliefs.

Few Hospitals, Few Schools

The government provides free education, but there are not enough teachers or schools, especially in rural areas. Many children stay at home to help their parents care for animals or grow food. For students who do manage to finish their schooling, there are three universities, at Conakry, Kankan, and Faranah.

Many infectious diseases and dangerous parasites thrive in Guinea's warm, wet climate, but the Guinean government does not have enough money to run a national health service or to provide drainage systems and clean drinking water. There are also very few hospitals, doctors, and nurses. Together, these facts make Guinea an unhealthy place to live. A baby born in Guinea today can expect to live for about forty-six years, but one baby in eight dies before its first birthday. Many Guinean women undergo the surgical procedure called female genital cutting (see SOMALIA).

Everyday Life

Conakry, the capital city of Guinea, is as busy, noisy, dirty, and full of crime as many other cities worldwide. It has modern office towers, elegant estates, fashionable hotels, traffic jams, nightclubs, and crowded slums where families live in huts made of rough concrete blocks roofed with metal sheets.

Conakry is not typical of the whole country. Most Guineans do not live in cities and hardly ever visit them. Instead, four out of every five live in the countryside and earn their living from the land. Many are subsistence farmers, growing enough for their families to eat, building their own houses (usually out of sun-dried mud and straw, roofed with straw thatch), making their own tools, and selling (or exchanging) any surplus produce for essentials, such as clothes or soap, that they cannot make themselves.

The crops they grow vary from region to region; rice grows well in the rainy lowlands close to the coast, while peanuts and cassava ripen in forest clearings. Plantains, coffee, cocoa, pineapples, and oil palms are grown in many lowland areas

Many Guinean women walk to local markets every day, carrying fresh fruits and vegetables from their family farms and gardens to sell.

alongside mangoes and bananas. In the mountains and on the savanna grasslands, farmers keep herds of cattle and goats. Oranges, avocados, beans, and other vegetables grow well in mountain gardens.

The food is plain and simple, though it can be very tasty. Most food is grown, harvested, cooked, sold, and served by women. This takes up a large part of their time. Everyday meals are based on boiled starchy foods such as rice, yams, and cassava, served with a thick sauce, usually made of chopped cassava leaves or sweet potato leaves, and pounded peanuts. Sometimes other vegetables are added. In towns people often buy their main meal, eaten in late morning, from take-out food stalls. Meat is for wealthy people or for special occasions. In towns beef and mutton are the most common meats; in villages, especially in rain forest areas, many different wild animals, including bush rat and monkey, are hunted and cooked for food. For dessert there is fruit.

Drinks include palm wine, soft drinks, sour milk thickened with cassava, and imported beer, tea, and coffee.

Riches from the Earth

There is not much industry in Guinea; only one person in ten works in a factory or a mine. However, the country has rich deposits of valuable minerals, especially bauxite, which can be processed to make aluminum. The hills and mountains in Guinea's southern rain forest region contain almost one-third of the world's bauxite, along with massive amounts of iron ore, plus diamonds and gold.

Fishers and their boats on the Niger River at dusk. They sail in pirogues, dugout boats carved from a single log, and plank boats, boats made from strips of wood nailed together.

All these minerals should make Guinea rich, but it is one of the poorest countries in the world. It must rely on aid from foreign governments, especially France. Because foreign companies jointly own the bauxite mines, Guinea makes very little profit from the mines. Gold and diamonds are often smuggled out of the country, thus avoiding taxes; Guinea gets no benefit from smuggled goods at all. The best sites for new iron mines are located in the middle of the rain forest; to make use of them, Guinea would have to destroy a precious natural environment and face hostility from foreign governments, which may result in less aid.

There are other economic problems that make Guinea poor. Transportation is slow, costly, and dangerous; in the rainy season many roads are flooded or knee-deep in

Beside the River

The great Niger River, over 2,500 miles (4,000 kilometers) long, flows through Guinea toward the sea. It rises in the rain forest and is home to an array of wildlife, including snakes, crocodiles, and hippopotamuses. Few forest people live close to its banks because the river often floods in the rainy season and houses would be swept away. However, fishers set up camps by the riverside in October and November, after the rains have finished. They dry the fish they catch and hang them over smoky fires to preserve them for later in the year. Where the river reaches the lowlands and gets closer to the sea, the rain forests end and fields and farms flourish on the riverbanks. The river is over a half mile (0.8 kilometers) wide here and less likely to cause damage by floods. However, boats have to take care to avoid stretches of shallow water, especially in the dry season.

mud. Wars in neighboring countries have made trade difficult. Guinea now has enormous debts to foreign bankers and has to use mining profits to help pay for them.

Praising Chiefs and Cattle

In spite of the hardships they face, Guinean people enjoy music and dancing. Malinke musicians are the most respected in Guinea and the neighboring lands. They play the *kora* (KOE-rah), an African instrument that is sometimes described as a mixture of harp and guitar. It has twenty-one strings and a sounding chamber made of a gourd the size of a soccer ball, which is cut in half and covered with a cowhide skin, like a drum. It creates a magical sound and it is very difficult to play. The Malinke also play slit-drums (made from hollow logs), and the *balafon* (BAH-lah-fawn), a large xylophone

A musician playing the kora. Traditionally this stringed instrument was played by singers and storytellers who passed their skills from generation to generation.

with empty gourds underneath that amplify the sound. Fulani shepherds are famous for flute playing and for their songs in praise of their cattle.

Many Malinke musicians are also *jalis* (JAH-lihs), traditional storytellers who retell ancient myths and legends. They memorize the past history of their people and pass it on to the next generation by word of mouth. Traditionally they also compose praise-songs to celebrate joyful occasions such as weddings or to honor powerful, important people. In the past this meant chiefs and village leaders; today it includes politicians and top civil servants as well. Popular jalis can also play a part in politics by expressing the views of ordinary people in their songs and by praising or criticizing government plans. The most famous praise-singers are women. Often the powerful people they praise richly reward them with presents.

Mory Kante

Mory Kante is Guinea's most famous music star. He was born around 1950 to a Malinke family of jalis and musicians. From the age of seven, he was trained to play the kora, but he wanted to experiment as well as play traditional songs. So he started a band in which Western-style brass instruments and an electric piano are played alongside the kora. His songs mix pounding rock music and sweet, tuneful soul music with African words and rhythms. He calls this fusion "African Funk."

Mory Kante now lives and makes recordings in France. Some traditional musicians strongly disapprove of his mixture of old and new, but his music is popular in many parts of the world.

Glossary

AIDS: *a*cquired *i*mmuno*d*eficiency *s*yndrome, a normally fatal disease often passed on by sexual intercourse. It is caused by the virus HIV (*h*uman *i*mmunodeficiency *v*irus), which attacks the body's ability to resist disease and infection.

bauxite: a mineral from which aluminum is made.

cassava: a plant with fleshy tuber roots, used as a food.

CFA franc: franc de la Communauté Financière Africaine (franc of the African Financial Community). This is a unit of currency shared by various African countries that were formerly French colonies.

circumcise: to remove a small piece of skin (the foreskin) from the penis of a boy or man.

communism: a theory that suggests that all property belongs to the community and that work should be organized for the common good.

   communist: someone who believes in the theory of communism.

compulsory: enforced, often by law.

coup: a change of government brought about by force.

estuary: the place where a river flows into a larger body of water.

expatriate: someone who lives in a country that is not his or her own; someone who withdraws allegiance to their native country.

feudal system: an ancient system in which peasants were allowed to live on and farm land owned by the rich nobles. In return for land and protection by the nobles, peasants worked and fought in times of war for the nobles.

filigree: delicate jewelry made from threads and beads, usually of gold or silver.

floodplain: a low-lying area that is regularly flooded by water.

franchise: a license to operate a business.

guinea fowls: birds the size of large chickens with handsome black and white feathers.

homage: the act of paying respect or allegiance, sometimes with money or gifts.

human rights abuses: human rights are conditions that many people believe are deserved by all human beings, such as freedom, equality, or justice. Abuses are acts that deny people such rights. Examples of abuses might include torture, censorship, or imprisonment without trial.

icon: an image of a holy person, often painted on wood and used mostly in Orthodox Christian worship

landlocked: having no access to the ocean; surrounded by other countries.

litters: decorated seats or beds on which important people were carried.

millet: a hardy cereal crop grown for food, drink, and fodder.

mutton: sheep meat

plantain: a fruit similar to the banana. It is a staple food in many tropical countries.

polytechnic institute: a place where many different subjects concerning science and technology are studied.

possession by spirits: a state where someone's body is controlled, or their personality is taken over, by an unseen being.

private enterprise: a business belonging to one person or a small group of people.

protectorate: a territory that is given the protection of a more powerful state. In the colonial period in Africa the "protection" was often just a ploy by European countries to achieve political control of the territory.

referendum: the chance to vote on important or controversial matters.

regalia: ceremonial objects, such as crowns, jewelry, or swords, belonging to rulers or other powerful people.

regime: a form of government.

republic: a country in which power rests with the people and their elected representatives. A president usually heads a republic.

rigged: dishonestly operated; fixed.

savanna: a grassland dotted with trees and drought-resistant undergrowth.

schistosomiasis: a tropical disease also known as bilharzia. It is caused by parasites that are passed on to humans in water contaminated by sewage. The disease causes fever, weight loss, anemia, and damage to the liver, intestines, and bladder.

sorghum: a grain crop commonly grown in hot countries.

squatter settlements: unplanned and overcrowded areas of housing, where poor people make simple shelters on land they do not own.

Further Reading

Internet Sites
Look under Countries A to Z in the Atlapedia Online Web Site at
    http://www.atlapedia.com/online/countries
Look under country listing in the CIA World Factbook Web Site at
    http://www.odci.gov/cia/publications/factbook
Look under country listing in the Library of Congress Country Studies Web Site at
    http://lcweb2.loc.gov/frd/cs/cshome.html

Ethiopia
Gish, Steven. *Ethiopia.* Tarrytown, NY: Benchmark Books, 1996.
Glaser, Elizabeth, and Brian McGovern. *Ethiopian Famine.* San Diego, CA: Lucent Books, 1990.
Kutz, Jane. *Ethiopia: The Roof of Africa.* Minneapolis, MN: Dillon Press, 1991.
Stewart, Gail. *Ethiopia.* New York: Crestwood House, 1991.

Gabon
Aniakor, Chike C. *Fang.* New York: Rosen Group, 1996.

Gambia
Ndukwe, Pat I. *Fulani.* New York: Rosen Group, 1995.
Nwanunobi, C. O. *Malinke.* New York: Rosen Group, 1996.
Sallah, Tijan M. *Wolof.* New York: Rosen Group, 1996.
Zimmermann, Robert. *The Gambia.* Danbury, CT: Children's Press, 1994.

Ghana
Akyea, E. Ofori. *Ewe.* New York: Rosen Group, 1996.
Barnett, Jeanie M. *Ghana.* Broomall, PA: Chelsea House, 1997.
Boateng, Faustine Ama. *Asante.* New York: Rosen Group, 1996.
Brace, Steve. *Ghana.* Detroit, MI: Thomson Learning, 1995.
Okeke, Chika. *Fante.* New York: Rosen Group, 1997.

Guinea
Ndukwe, Pat I. *Fulani.* New York: Rosen Group, 1995.
Nwanunobi, C. O. *Malinke.* New York: Rosen Group, 1996.

Index

Abaume, Jean-Hilaire, 190
Accra, Ghana, *200*, 210
Adae Festival, 202
Adal, 173–74
Addis Ababa, Ethiopia, 184–85, *185*
Adweneasa, 212
Afan Oromo, 177
Afar, 178, *178*, 180, 183
Akan, 205–6
Akosombo Dam, Ghana, 203–4
Aksum Empire, 171–72, *172*
Aku, 196, 197, 199
Amhara, 175, 177, 184
Amharic language, 177
Anuak, 178, 183
Arabic: in Ethiopia, 178; in Guinea, 220
Arts and crafts: in Ethiopia, 186, *186*; in Gabon, *193*; in Ghana, 212, *212*
Asantehene, 201
Ashanti, 201–3, 205, 206, 207, *207*, 210–11, 212, *213*
Askenkee, 210
Athletics in Ethiopia, 186

Baka, 188
Balafon, 223
Banjul, Gambia, 196, 198
Bantu-speakers, 188, 189, 192–93
Benachin, 199
Benge, 193
Berbere, 185–86
Bieri, *193*
Bongo, Albert-Bernard (Omar), 190, *190*, 193
British people: in Gambia, 196; in Ghana, 202–3

Catholics: in Ethiopia, 174, 177, 178; in Gabon, 193
Chat, 187
Christians: in Gambia, 197; in Ghana, 207; in Guinea, 220. *See also* Catholics, Protestants
Clothing: in Ethiopia, *177*, *179*, *180*, 183, 184, 187; in Gambia, *199*
Conakry, Guinea, 220–21
Conté, Lansana, 217–18, 219

Dagomba, in Ghana, 202, 205, *205*, 213
Dance: in Gambia, *199*; in Ghana, 213
Domoda, 199
Dutch people in Ghana, 202
Dyula, 220

Education: in Ethiopia, 181; in Gabon, 192; in Gambia, 197–98; in Ghana, 211–13; in Guinea, *219*, 220, *220*
Elmina, Ghana, *203*
English language: in Ethiopia, 178; in Gambia, 197; in Ghana, 205

Eshira, 193
Ewe, 201, 203, 205, 206, 212, 213

Falasha, 180
Fang language, 192
Fang people, 189, 192–93
Fante, 202–3, 205, 206, 210
Farming: in Ethiopia, 181, 182, *182*, 183; in Gambia, 198, 199; in Ghana, 208–9, *208*; in Guinea, 221
Festivals: in Ethiopia, *173*, 187, *187*; in Ghana, 202, 207, *207*, 208
Fishing: in Gambia, 198–99; in Ghana, 208; in Guinea, 222, *222*
Food: in Ethiopia, 185–86, *185*; in Gabon, 191, *191*; in Gambia, 199; in Ghana, 209–10, *209*; in Guinea, 221–22, *221*
Fouta Djallon, Guinea, 215
Franceville, Gabon, 190
French Equatorial Africa, 190
French language: in Gabon, 192; in Guinea, 219–20, *219*
French people: in Gabon, 190; in Guinea, 215–17, *216*
French West Africa, 216
Fufu, 191
Fulani: in Gambia, 195–96, *195*, 197, 215; in Guinea, 217, 218–19, 223

Ga-Adangme, 205
Gabata, 186
Ga languages, 205
Gambia River, Gambia, 198, *198*
Geez, 172, 177, 180
Ghana Empire, 195, 215
Ghazi, Ahmad ibn Ibrahim al, 174
Gold Coast, 203
Gonja, 205
Griots, 199
Gurage, 178, 184

Haile Selassie, Emperor of Ethiopia, 175
Hanno, 194
Harer, Ethiopia, 184, *184*
Hareri, 178, 184
Health care: in Ethiopia, 181, *181*; in Gabon, 192; in Gambia, 198; in Ghana, 211, *211*; in Guinea, 220
Herodotus, 194
Highlife, 213
Horseracing in Ethiopia, 186
Housing: in Ethiopia, 183, 184–85, *184*; in Gabon, 191; in Ghana, 210–11, *210*; in Guinea, *218*, 220–21

Industry: in Ethiopia, 181; in Gambia, 198; in Guinea, 222
Injera, 185, *185*

Italians in Ethiopia, 175

Jalis, 223
Jammeh, Yahya, 196
Jawara, Dawda, 196
Jews in Ethiopia, 180
Jola, 197

Kante, Mory, 223
Kelewele, 210
Kenkey, 209
Kente cloth, 212, *212*
Khruschev, Nikita, *217*
Kissi, 216, 219
Kola nut, 192
Koma, 219
Kongo, 189
Kora, 199, 223, *223*
Kota, 189, 193
Kpelle, 219
Krakro, 210
Kumasi, Ghana, 201, 202

Labé, Guinea, 215
Lalibela, Ethiopia, 173, *173*
Languages: in Ethiopia, 177, 178; in Gabon, 192; in Gambia, 197; in Ghana, 202, 205; in Guinea, 219–20, *219*
Libreville, Gabon, 190, 191–92, *192*
Limann, Hilla, 204
Loango Kingdom, 188
Loma, 219

Mali Empire, 195, 215
Malinke: in Gambia, 195, 196, 197, 199; in Guinea, 215, 216, 218, 219, 223
Mamprusi, 202
Mandingo, 195
Mandinka. *See* Malinke
Mariam, Mengistu Haile, 176
Maskal, 187
M'ba, Léon, 190
Mbete, 193
Menelik II, Emperor of Ethiopia, 174, 175
Mengistu Haile Mariam, 176
Mining: in Ethiopia, 181; in Gabon, 191; in Ghana, 203, 209; in Guinea, 222
Mole-Dagbani, 205
Mole languages, 202, 205
More languages, 202
Mpongwe, 189, 190, 192, 193
Music: in Gabon, 193; in Gambia, 199, *199*; in Ghana, 213, *213*; in Guinea, 223, *223*
Muslims: in Ethiopia, 173, 177, 178, 180, *180*; in Gambia, *194*, 197; in Ghana, 207; in Guinea, 215, 220
Myene, 189, 192

Page numbers in *italic* indicate illustrations.

Niger River, Guinea, 222, *222*
Nkrumah, Kwame, 203–4
Nuer, in Ethiopia, 178, 183, *183*

Odwira Festival, 207, *207*
Okomfo Anokye Sword, 202
Oromo, 175, *176*, 177, 180, 184
Orthodox Church, 172, 173, *173*, 177,
  178–80, *179*, 187, *187*
Orungu, 189, 192
Osei Tutu, Chief, 201

Panu, in Gabon, 193
Pito, 210
Pomdo statues, 219
Portuguese people: in Ethiopia, 174; in
  Gambia, 196; in Ghana, 202
Protestants: in Ethiopia, 177, 178; in
  Gabon, 193

Rashaida, *180*
Rawlings, Jerry, 204, *204*
Religions: in Ethiopia, 172, 173, *173*,
  174, 177, 178–80, 187, *187*; in Gabon,
  193, *193*; in Gambia, *194*, 197; in
  Ghana, 207–8; in Guinea, 215, 220

Roba, Fatuma, 186

Seke, 193
Selassie, Haile, 175
Selassie, Haile Gebre, 186
Senegambia, 195–96
Serahuli, 195, 197, *197*
Serer, 195, 197
Shemma, *177*, 183
Sidama, 178
Slave trade: in Gabon, 189, 190; in
  Gambia, 196; in Ghana, 202; in
  Guinea, 215
Soccer: in Ethiopia, *185*, 186; in
  Gambia, 199
Somali in Ethiopia, 177, 178
Songhai Empire, 215
Soninke, 195
Sports and games: in Ethiopia, *185*, 186;
  in Gambia, 199
Susu, 215, 218, 219

Tabot, 179–80
Tafari, Ras, 175
Tej, 186
Teke, 193

Tewodros, Emperor of Ethiopia, 174–75
Tigre, 175, 176, 177, *177*
Tigrinya, 177
Timbo, Guinea, 215
Timkat, *173*, 187, *187*
Touré, Ahmed Sekou, 216–17, *217*, 219
Touré, Samori, 216, *216*
Tourism in Gambia, 198
Tozafi, 209
Tukuls, 183
Tutu, Osei, 201

Vili, 188
Volta, Lake; Ghana, 203–4

Wat, 185–86
Wolof, 195, 197, 199
Wrestling: in Ethiopia, 186; in Gambia,
  199

Yohannis IV, Emperor of Ethiopia, 174,
  175

Zauditu, Empress of Ethiopia, 175

Page numbers in *italic* indicate illustrations.